Wolf's Inferno

Other books by Craig MacIntosh

The Fortunate Orphans
(Beaver's Pond Press, 2009)

The Last Lightning
(Beaver's Pond Press, 2013)

McFadden's War
(Pugio Books, 2015)

Wolf's Vendetta
(Pugio Books, 2015)

WOLF'S

INFERNO

ISBN: 978-0-9913611-4-4

Cover design by Kent Mackintosh
Book design by Belldog Media and typeset in Janson Text

Printed in the United States of America
First Printing: 2016

19 18 17 16   5 4 3 2 1 0

Published by Pugio Books
13607 Crosscliffe Place
Rosemount, MN 55068
www.cjmacintosh.com

ACKNOWLEDGEMENTS

Another book, and another debt to my collaborative team. Editor, Cindy Rogers, put her usual perfect touches to my words. Without her input there would be no coherent story. While writing *Wolf's Inferno* I relied on Sergeant William Patrick Murphy, a detective with the San Diego Police Department's Narcotics Unit, to keep my investigative details authentic.

Brian Cristofono, St. Paul Fire Department EMT, explained a first responder's on site role. Thanks to brother Kent Mackintosh for the striking cover artwork as always, Jeff Wechter, who handled the interior, and Molly Miller's proofreading skills. I continue to mine both retired Navy SEAL Chuck Wolf's store of adventure tales, and former FBI Special Agent Jerry DeWees's forensics expertise. My indebtedness includes gratitude to Linda for her indefatigable support.

"Surely wickedness burns like a fire..."
—Isaiah 9:18

To the members of the San Diego Police Department Street Gang Unit—holding the line like so many of their fellow officers across this nation.

Chapter 1

Quezon City, Philippines, 1995

His prey was late. Not unexpected, nor a complication. Sparrow had time. Having arrived early, he took up a mid-block position opposite the hotel's entrance. To passersby, the handsome young man wearing sunglasses and a cream-colored linen suit and tie might have been a student between exams, a newly minted lawyer or businessman on the cusp of success. Perhaps he was only some nameless cog in the machinery of a government office where, for want of a bribe, backlogged files spilled from dusty drawers. To his left, a stolen Vespa, freshly repainted as part of its disguise, was parked at the curb within reach. Its mobility would make things easier, allow him to take to sidewalks if need be, to use narrow garbage-strewn alleys branching from the busy street if things got dicey. He had memorized four escape routes as a precaution.

He sat quietly in the banyan's shade, spooning *iskrambol*—shaved ice topped with caramelized brown sugar—his favorite street vendor treat, the only happy remnant of childhood.

Nineteen years before, Sparrow had seen his father, mother and an uncle gunned down in front of him during a raid by the army and police. The trauma, first of many, seared his soul. *Always remember*, his older sister told him. *Never forget. Seek revenge. See justice done if it takes a lifetime.* Four years later, this same unforgiving sister died in a hail of bullets during a government-sanctioned assassination. Though he witnessed her murder from his hiding place in a closet, he had not known that it came with an official stamp of approval. His one surviving family member, a distant cousin who took him in, recited all of this until Sparrow had memorized the family's canonized version of events.

At sixteen, at his cousin's urging, he killed his first man, a corrupt low-level government official. It had been easy. His youth had made him invisible. The next year, he added two more, a Chinese gambler and a British ex-pat oilman, both deeply in debt to the wrong people. After that, he was on his own, alighting here and there, picking up assignments when he needed money, but never aligning himself with any one of metro Manila's hundreds of criminal gangs. As part of his disguise, Sparrow eschewed tattoos in order to travel unblemished in different worlds. Sometimes disguised as a seminarian, student, or wealthy scion he easily moved within Manila society's fiercely competitive strata with no one the wiser.

A chameleon, he floated incognito through the criminal netherworld as well. Only his aging cousin knew his real name. When a need for Sparrow's skills arose, he would get a call and an assignment from his relative, who took a small cut.

What had begun as message drops in Manila shops and street kiosks had given way to new technology. Sparrow had adapted, giving up the drops and cash for disposable cellphones, anonymous emails, and hidden bank accounts. Long after his cousin died, Sparrow kept his anonymity as his score rose. He remained a cipher to police, a myth. A *multo*—a ghost who killed.

Today, in the plaza adjacent to the hotel, under the banyan's leafy canopy, it would be no different. He was there to kill a man, an American targeted for sins, real or imagined. *Perhaps my client is a cuckolded husband or defrauded business partner who wants this man dead. No matter. I will spare the girl, however, if she does not interfere.*

Sparrow spotted his prey exiting the colonial-era hotel with a laughing Filipina voluptuary on his arm. There was no mistaking the pale, plump, balding target. Tossing what remained of his treat, Sparrow brushed his hands against the linen jacket, straddled the Vespa, and kicked it into life.

Sparrow patted the handgun in his waistband where it could be easily grasped, yet was still hidden by his unbuttoned jacket. With his right hand managing the throttle, it would be a left-handed shot, not the easiest, but one Sparrow had made before. He would close the distance to his target before he fired and he would not miss.

Rocking forward off the kickstand, Sparrow gunned the scooter directly at the oblivious couple. Sparrow pulled the automatic from his waistband, holding it at arm's length as he drew abreast of the pair. Pausing on the hotel's marble steps, the American turned at the scooter's sound, his mouth open in mid-sentence, surprise in his eyes at the gun's muzzle six feet away. The woman screamed.

POP, POP, POP!

Sparrow pumped three shots into his victim's chest and fled.

The American fell like a stone at the woman's feet, his blood splattering her shoes. Bystanders dropped to the sidewalk or flattened themselves against buildings, covering their faces as the Vespa roared past.

Weaving between stalled traffic, Sparrow disappeared into an alley.

Chapter 2

Tondo District, Manila, present day

Buzzing like an angry hive, the capital city's most dangerous quarter pulsed with life. Steaming with humidity from a late-afternoon downpour, narrow streets swarmed with those driven from their burrows by boredom or the evening's heat. They came, perching on battered plastic chairs or wood planks—families, beggars, the dispossessed and the jobless—gathering on crumbling sidewalks.

Drawn like moths to a flame, Manila's poorest of the poor ate, drank, gossiped, and gambled amidst an endless parade of nightlife. People gawked at the show from street-level hovels, bars, or rickety rooming house balconies draped with laundry. In Tondo's labyrinth, exhausted mothers put hungry children to bed on sheets of flattened cardboard spread across dirt floors. Roosters sat on thresholds. Skinny dogs roamed at will, snapping at each other over scraps.

Gangsters, addicts, informers, con artists, and whores trolled the streets, baiting their traps in dark doorways or Tondo's infamous, claustrophobic alleys. Alert to the scent of innocents or the gullible, gang members and pickpockets prowled at all hours, virtually immune to police because of the city's notorious gridlock.

Flooded in low spots from the earlier rain, broken pavement was choked with a line of jeepneys, pedicabs, and motorbikes sitting in hubcap-deep water. Squealing in joy, tribes of barefoot feral children chased each other through fetid pools. Wading pedestrians shouldering their most precious dry belongings sought higher ground.

A black SUV bulled its way down the street, scattering slow-moving cyclists, street vendors, and the unwary with blasts from its horn. Curious sidewalk patrons squatting around a charcoal grill set on blocks glanced at the shiny car with the tinted windows. A vacant-eyed street peddler, holding a string of sandals in one hand, bagged fruit in the other, stared at the passing machine. Shirtless men playing pool under flickering fluorescent lights interrupted their game long enough to gaze at the big vehicle carving a wake in the puddles. Without being told, they knew who was behind the dark windows.

The black car drove on, stopping on damp pavement just short of the next corner. Overhead, a tangled spider web of pirated power lines draped a three-story concrete building between sagging wooden tenements topped with peeling billboards. On the tall building's flat roof, armed men leaned over the parapet like gargoyles, staring at the idling car in the street. The last of the bosses had arrived.

Below the lookouts, four large tattooed men with shaved heads and beefy hairless shoulders stood statue-like at the top of stone steps leading to a pair of iron doors wearing flaking yellow paint. Despite the heat, the building's first-level windows were shuttered. Having been told to expect the visitors, the wary quartet gripped handguns, their precaution instinctive.

The SUV's driver lowered his window and signaled. One of the four nodded and opened the metal doors. Two unsmiling bodyguards got out of the car. One held the back door for a slender man wearing a spotless khaki safari jacket and trousers. The second guard, his eyes focused on the street, backpedaled to the steps and took up his post. The man in khaki and his bodyguard trotted up the stairs past the watchdogs and disappeared behind the iron doors.

The two climbed to the second floor where more men with guns waited in a dim, peeling hallway. One of the posted thugs opened a door for the small man in khaki. He entered a vaulted room thick with cigar smoke. Despite laboring overhead fans, a bluish layer hovered, obscuring the ceiling. The room seemed too small for the large, round mahogany table sitting in the middle of the parquet floor.

At the table sat three men—all notorious gangsters well-known to Manila's police and media: Jose *"JuJu"* Cruz, government insider and undisputed master of the legion of bagmen working the capital's *jueteng* racket, the addictive illegal numbers game; Rodolfo *"Chito"* Ferrer, Tondo's prostitution and smuggling czar; and Bonifacio *"Bonny"* Pineda, king of all black market electronics and DVD piracy. Grunts of recognition filled the air as the late arrival, Alberto *"Razor"* Mendoza, entered the room and took the fourth chair.

JuJu Cruz, the evening's host and, at 265 pounds, the largest among the quartet of crime bosses, greeted the man in khaki. "Eh, Razor, you come all this way to grace us with your presence. What an honor you give us, eh?"

The salutation was partly affectionate and partly a jesting goad. Both men knew, as did the others at the table, that Mendoza, Zamboangan drug dealer and arms smuggler, detested the nickname bestowed during his youth as a merciless enforcer on these same streets. Now acting as *Papa Manong*—head boss of Mindanao's notorious *Kuratong Baleleng*—Mendoza was a man on a mission.

A snap of the host's fingers and a bottle of Tanduay rum was brought to the table by a silent server. JuJu Cruz had him pour four tumblers on a silver platter and circle the table, serving each man in turn. Grinning broadly, JuJu made a toast. *"Mabuhay!* To success tonight, eh?"

Smiling, Mendoza raised his glass with the others but did not down the rum.

Cruz said, "Eh, Razor, my rum is not to your liking?"

"Forgive me, JuJu. These days even the finest rum is poison to my system. But I salute your generosity, regardless."

Cruz took the fiery rum in one gulp. "Ah, of course, I forget, my friend. Perhaps you prefer a juice...or milk?"

The remark drew nervous chuckles from the other men, then silence.

With silence came tension, but Mendoza dismissed the slight with a smile and a wave of his hand. "A fine rum, JuJu, but as you know, I did not come to drink toasts." He nodded to the three bosses, spread his bony hands on the table, and said, "You have before you my proposal to seek your assistance in righting a wrong—correcting an insult to my *barkada*, my family. You know the circumstances. You are obligated to assist me as surely as I would honor such a request from you. Were the problem yours I would spare no effort to see your honor restored regardless of cost. Agreed?"

The men signaled agreement with guttural sounds and a collective shaking of heads. Another round was poured and downed, the glasses hitting the table in unison.

"At this moment consider your problem ours," growled Bonny Pineda, a barrel-shaped gangster, his lips parted in a theatrical sneer. He looked around the table for approval and got it.

The pimp, Chito Ferrer, his sloping shoulders hunched, stood, slurring his words, "By all means. We mus' show solidarity, Razor. We...with you." He sat down with some effort, rocking back and forth as if he were about to topple. "Yes, I'm in," he added.

Slamming his fist on the table, his eyes blazing, JuJu Cruz rose to his feet. "You have heard our council. We agree with your plan for revenge. The insult will be avenged. You have only to ask. Tell us how we can stand with you."

"Your words of support, your endorsement, give me heart," said Mendoza. "My needs are simple. I need one man. A very special man. His English must be flawless. He must know how to kill an enemy without drawing attention to himself. He will be sent on a distant mission and must keep his wits about him among strangers. He will be handsomely rewarded if successful. If he fails and is caught, yet does not break, he will be well taken care of. He must be silent. Deadly. Do you know of such a man?"

The description brought silence to the table. The server padded about the table refilling the glasses. Mendoza covered his tumbler with a hand as the man passed.

"This is a city full of men who have one or more of these talents," said Cruz, stroking his mustache. "To embody them all...ah, that will take time. Is not impossible, of course. How much time you give us?"

Mendoza couched his request as a challenge of honor. "Surely, among the three of you, there must be such a man," he purred. "I've searched my own ranks and regretfully, have not found this man. As you know, my situation in Zamboanga is somewhat difficult at the moment. That is why I find myself in this city, at this table, with you, brothers. I can give you two days. It is a matter of pride."

"We will find you such a man," vowed Cruz. "You will have your revenge. It will not be cheap, my friend."

"What price honor? Of course I am prepared to consider such costs."

Declining the trio's invitation to stay longer, Mendoza excused himself. He did not completely trust these men. Nor they him. He slipped into the corridor and signaled his bodyguard to follow. The pair went down the stairs, out into the night where their SUV waited.

Chapter 3

Twenty-four hours later JuJu Cruz sent word to Mendoza that he had found the man the gang boss from Zamboanga needed. Cruz suggested they meet at a neutral spot: a small open-air restaurant on the edge of Tondo. Mendoza arrived early, parked in the shade of an ancient towering banyan, and sent a bodyguard to scout the location. Reassured that the place Cruz had selected was not the site of an ambush, Mendoza took a table at the rear of the open-sided café and ordered a pot of green tea. He placed two envelopes next to the ceramic pot and waited.

Cruz arrived in a black armored SUV with a bodyguard and the killer he had recruited for Mendoza. The bodyguard took up his post from which he could keep an eye on the street and Mendoza's man, who was equally suspicious of his opposite number. Cruz and companion took seats at Mendoza's table.

"Ah, I present *ang maya*—The Sparrow," Cruz said. "The man you seek." Cruz nodded at the young, effeminate-looking man on his left.

Mendoza studied the stranger without smiling. Slight of build, with long hair and longer eyelashes, his soft round face deceptively innocent, the would-be assassin looked more university student than killer. The faint beginnings of a mustache outlined full lips. Only the eyes were hard, a pitilessness about them.

"You have a name?"

"Sparrow will do."

"A man of few words," said Cruz, wagging a finger. "Few words but many talents. He'll need money," Cruz said. "Such a job is expensive, you know."

Mendoza pointed at the larger of the two envelopes. "The money is here."

"And for my courtesy in finding such a skilled gentleman?"

Mendoza pushed a slimmer envelope at the gangster. "Your fee, JuJu."

Cruz pocketed the envelope without looking at its contents. He signaled a server. A nervous reed-thin youth brought a bottle of rum and three tumblers to the table. Cruz dismissed him and poured for each of them.

Mendoza, his eyes on Sparrow, pushed away his glass. The assassin locked eyes with him and did likewise.

A good sign, thought Mendoza. *One not given to drink.*

Cruz raised his glass in a toast. "*Mabuhay.*" He swallowed the liquid fire. "Such seriousness, my friends. This is a time for celebration. We have concluded an arrangement. All parties are satisfied, yet I find myself drinking alone. Ah, well. So be it." He corralled their untouched glasses. "To success."

Cruz downed their rum, then rose, signaling his bodyguard. "My part is done. I leave you to your details."

Shadowed by his watchdog, Cruz swaggered away. Mendoza and his new hire watched him go.

"Ah, now to business," said Mendoza. "Your English is good, yes?"

"Good enough."

"I want a man who can fit in once he reaches America. Can you do that?"

"I have been there twice before."

"I seek a particular man there. Once you find him, I want him killed."

A nod and a faint boyish smile.

"Killing is easy," said Mendoza, his voice flat. "It's what comes in its wake that is sometimes difficult. That will not be easy but you will be well rewarded."

"I understand."

"When can you do this for me?"

"Yesterday."

Mendoza dismissed the bravado. "Arrogance is not a skill."

"True. Forgive me, but do not mistake my confidence for arrogance, sir."

"Perhaps," said Mendoza. "However, the man I want killed is a warrior. He is dangerous. He is no fool."

"I understand," said Sparrow.

"Mendoza folded his hands in front of him. "JuJu assures me you have done such work before."

A nod and a subtle Cheshire grin. "Your schedule for killing this man?"

"I wish it done within a fortnight, though the actual timing is best left to you."

Glancing around as if to avoid being overheard, Sparrow folded his hands in front of him as though to pray. "What arrangements have you made?"

Mendoza poured himself a cup of tea. "You are to fly to Hawaii posing as a businessman. Once you have selected your flight, call me. There is a man here in Manila who will create a passport and papers for you. My people in Honolulu will meet your flight and alert me when you arrive. They will have additional funds for you and will furnish you with new identification. From there, you board a domestic flight to San Diego, thus avoiding the problem of customs."

"I understand. Please continue."

"You have only to follow the travel plans as instructed. The rest will be up to you. You will be well paid for your success."

Mendoza slid the thick envelope across the table. "All you need to know is in there. Names, phone numbers, contacts, and money. Once you reach California you will be met at the airport and driven to a safe house. Our friends will provide you with a choice of weapons."

"Papa Manong, permit me to interrupt, if I might."

"What is this?" said Mendoza. "I warn you. If you seek to change the terms you will not find me agreeable."

"Of course not. The arrangement stands. But I must confess to you that the situation changed within the last hour."

Mendoza bristled. "You take me for a fool?" He got to his feet and signaled his bodyguard.

Sparrow did not rise. "I have a concern, that is all."

Mendoza waved away his approaching driver and sat down. "Enough of this. You try my patience. Explain yourself but be careful with your words."

"Of course, sir. The arrangements you made will stand. I will honor the agreement we made."

"Then why this trick?"

"Is not a trick, sir. I agree to the contract. I apologize for the last-minute change, but it will be to our advantage, after all."

"'Our advantage?' How do I know I can trust you?"

"My reputation is my word."

"Is JuJu Cruz's hand in this?"

A shaking of the head. "You are wise, *Papa Manong*."

Mendoza's eyes narrowed at the young man across from him. "You tire me with your riddles and flattery. Explain yourself."

"*May paggalang, ginoo*—with respect, sir—how well do you know JuJu Cruz?"

Startled by the question, Mendoza repeated the query. "How well do I know JuJu Cruz? Who are you to ask this?"

"I meant no disrespect."

"So you say. But why would you ask such a thing?"

"I beg you to understand my dilemma."

Folding his gnarled hands, Mendoza said, "Very well. Explain."

"Do not be concerned, but I was given five thousand dollars to kill you."

Mendoza stiffened. "By whom?"

"JuJu Cruz requested my services, sir."

"And you tell me this? Why?"

"I never ask the reasons a person seeks my skills. It is only business, after all." Dark eyes fixed on the table, he waited for Mendoza to speak. A long pause, the older man's mind racing, his lined mahogany face fixed in a scowl.

"Well, this complicates things, does it not? One word from me and I could have you killed where you sit."

"I know this. No one would avenge me. I am nothing. But then, JuJu Cruz would replace me and the matter would then become your problem."

Drumming bony fingers on the table, Mendoza rasped, "Undoubtedly you have a proposition for me, correct?"

"I do," Sparrow said. "Match the sum JuJu Cruz promised and I kill him instead."

"Ah, why not ask for more to turn the tables on him?"

Tapping the envelope in front of him, Sparrow said, "Because you have paid for my services in America and I hold your money. You have only to match JuJu Cruz's fee and I will eliminate him prior to leaving for America."

Mendoza's eyes narrowed. "And I am to trust you?"

"My initial contract was with you. Like you, I am a man of honor. If you decline this offer two things will happen. First, I will go to America and find the man you've hired me to eliminate. When that is done I will return, obligated to fulfill my contract with JuJu Cruz."

"To kill me."

"Yes. Nothing personal, you understand."

"*IF* you return."

"I will return."

Another long pause. "Very well. I will match JuJu's offer but with one exception."

"Name it."

"You are to kill him before you leave Manila."

"*Walang problema*—not a problem."

The two rose together and shook hands. A crooked smile twisted Mendoza's lips as his fingers dug into Sparrow's softer flesh. "You should know that I was aware JuJu hired you to kill me. When I learned this I thought I would see how it played out with you."

Sparrow flashed a brief look of relief. "You are wise, Papa Manong."

Eyes narrowing, Mendoza stroked his chin. "Not so wise, cautious."

"Cautious, yes," Sparrow said. "If I may...the five thousand."

"Of course," said Mendoza. He waved over his driver and snapped his fingers. The gunman handed over a dog-eared envelope and retreated. Mendoza said, "Count it if you wish."

"No need." The younger man added the envelope to the others.

Mendoza said, "Under the circumstances, it sounds odd to say that I wanted to see what you would do. I had asked after your reputation beforehand. There is honor involved in these things sometimes."

"Always, sir."

"Though some would call it otherwise."

Mendoza gestured to his bodyguards in the background. "Had you not revealed JuJu's plan to me you would not have left our meeting alive."

The assassin shrugged. "There's always a risk in such doings. But then you would have been without my services for your revenge in America and vulnerable to your enemy here."

"I might have struck first to remove that threat."

"Leaving the American alive."

The two strolled together toward Mendoza's car. "Ah, true," he said, "but there are others willing. Some among our people in California."

"A gamble at best."

"Possibly. Know that I do not tolerate failure."

"Nor do I."

"Good. We understand each other."

Mendoza got into his car's back seat, a grim wizened figure settling behind tinted windows. He told his driver to wait. He watched Sparrow pocket the envelopes and then cross the crowded street to be swallowed by the crowd.

Chapter 4

Sparrow hurried through a winding maze dense with beggars, food carts, squalling infants, and pickpockets. Smoke from cooking fires, decaying meat and unwashed bodies filled his nostrils. He tasted the scent of incense heavy in the humid air. Stopping in a doorway, he looked back to see if he had been followed by one of Mendoza's men. Satisfied, he turned to go, but felt a tug on his trousers. He glanced down. A legless, toothless crone grinned up at him. Fleeing her outstretched hand, he ducked down a narrow side alley then picked up his pace, batting aside drying laundry and the pleading hands of hungry children. A bevy of whores cooed to him as he rushed past them.

He crossed a concrete arch spanning a sluggish canal choked with sewage and rotting garbage. On the other side, home: a three-story factory building since converted to one-room flats jammed with forty families. A fire marshal's nightmare, the overcrowded brick ark overlooked the canal. One last look behind him, and Sparrow took creaking wooden stairs, two steps at a time. He closed and locked the door of his second-floor quarters behind him.

Working quickly, he spilled the contents of the envelopes on his sagging mattress, separating the money from the airline vouchers and Mendoza's scrawled instructions. In one envelope, he placed one thousand crisp American dollars and set it aside. The remaining money went into a black nylon bag with the notes and flight schedules. He was now wealthier than his entire neighborhood. He hid the bag in his safe, a loose board pried from the wall above the doorframe.

Envelope in his pocket, Sparrow went down the hall to the communal washroom. Ignoring two tenants squatting in tiled stalls, he leaned over a zinc trough, turning a tap to splash water on his sweaty torso. He toweled off and changed into a clean shirt, then returned to the streets and hailed a cyclo taxi.

Twenty minutes later, mid-block on Narra Street, he exited at the front entrance of the Seng Guan Temple. Sparrow followed the Buddhist faithful through the high arched doorway. Noises from the street faded, yielding to the temple's serenity. Kneeling on low, red-cushioned benches, worshippers bowed before an altar of carved, gilded screens lined with bowls of yellow flowers.

Sparrow bypassed the supplicants and padded up the stairs to the second floor chanting room. At the far end of the red-columned, soaring atrium, hands clasped in prayer, four people on their knees whispered *sutras*—prayers— before a sculpted trio of golden Buddhas. Sparrow bowed in respect and slipped behind a hooded figure sitting cross-legged at the rear of the room, his back against one of the stout red columns.

"You are late," hissed the man.

"My apologies. Mendoza was particularly long-winded."

Rhythmic gong tones floated in the open stairwell. Chanting from the front of the room began, covering the pair's conversation.

"What did you learn?"

"Mendoza wants you to kill JuJu Cruz within the fortnight."

The hood turned, revealing a hint of profile—flat nose, a high furrowed cheekbone, and full lips. "Interesting. These men turn on each other like snakes. So be it. In the first note passed to me there was a mention of an American he wanted killed. Was I mistaken?"

"You were not. JuJu Cruz has been added to his request. He still wants you to hunt down this man in California."

"Ah, America. That will take some thought. Did he give you the money?"

"Yes, I brought it with me as you ordered."

"All of it?"

"What Mendoza gave me."

A wiry brown arm shot from the robe's sleeve, the hand open.

Sparrow placed the worn envelope in the waiting palm. The arm disappeared in the folds as the hooded man counted the money. "One thousand dollars?" he said. "Does he think I am a fool? This is not nearly enough to bring down a man like JuJu Cruz and kill the American."

"A good faith gesture from Mendoza. He promised five times that when Cruz is killed and ten times that when the American is dead."

An angry murmur. "Most unusual. Very well. I hold him to his promise. Now, about this American. Tell me everything you know."

"I am to be contacted with those details once Cruz is dead."

"What else did you learn?"

"That is all. Will I see you again?"

The hooded figure rose, bowed, and whispered. "Listen for news of JuJu Cruz's death. I will call for you. Then, I will go to America when the time is right."

"As you say." He bowed low to the floor, his forehead touching the cool marble, his eyes closed.

When he sat up, the man was gone. Sparrow got up and backed from the room. Though not a believer, he felt the stares from the gilded Buddhas follow him to the stairs.

Chapter 5

Coastline Training Range, San Diego

Retired Green Beret Sam McFadden sat at a twelve foot long counter feeding nine-millimeter rounds into a Beretta's magazine. Next to him, his wife Regina did the same, though without his enthusiasm and at a slower pace. He had loaded three to her one. McFadden glanced up, his concentration broken by the familiar sound of muffled gunfire from the indoor range behind thick tinted windows to his front. Three shooters with pistols were pumping rounds downrange into targets taped to cardboard silhouettes. The firing ceased. McFadden watched the trio retrieve their targets and compare their efforts.

"Bless the regulars," he said. "Good for business. May their tribe increase."

Arching an eyebrow, Reggie put down the half-filled magazine and looked at her husband. "Tell me again why I need to know how to use this gun?"

McFadden paused, his eyes on her. "We've been over this before, Reggie. Because...just in case. Like knowing how to swim or drive a stick shift."

"Sam, they don't make stick-shift cars anymore."

"Okay, maybe it's like knowing how to use Facebook or some such skill."

"Ha, you don't even use Facebook. Your staff does that for you." She batted her eyes. "Besides, that's a frivolous comparison. Facebook can't kill."

McFadden pushed another round in the magazine and placed it in a plastic tray. "True. But social media can ruin a person's reputation."

"And a handgun can ruin someone's life," she retorted.

"But Facebook won't save your life, Reggie." He patted the holstered Beretta 92FS at his hip. "This would."

She put down the magazine. "Damn, I just broke a nail. And you're to blame, Sam McFadden."

He reached for the magazine. "I'll finish loading. Sorry about the nail, but it's good for clients to see the owner's wife use the range once in a while."

"You say that every time you drag me down here."

"I'm not dragging you. Besides, you need to see where some of your money's going. Same for your mother's investment."

"Same old Sam. I only do this because I love you."

He smiled. "As good a reason as any."

McFadden fed the last rounds in the magazine. "Okay, Reggie. Let's find ourselves an open lane and kill some paper."

The two inserted foam earplugs and donned plastic safety glasses. They put on padded earmuffs and stepped through airlock doors to the firing range. They passed one of McFadden's employees working with a husband and wife team.

"We'll be on lane ten," said McFadden in passing.

"Roger that, Sam," said the instructor.

McFadden and Reggie went through a second soundproofed door, passed the three shooters they had seen earlier, and set up in the last lane. He flipped on the safety, inserted a fifteen-round magazine, pulled back the slide, and released it, chambering the first round. He lay the loaded Beretta on the lane's waist-high shelf, its muzzle pointed downrange. McFadden tore strips of masking tape from a roll at the station, taped a paper target to the cardboard backing on the overhead carrier, and sent it downrange seven yards.

At his invitation, Reggie, shiny long black hair tied in a ponytail, stepped to the lane's waist-high shelf. She stood with her left leg forward, the pistol gripped with both hands. She aimed at the silhouette suspended in front of her. Squinting at the orange rectangle centered in the outline, she squeezed the trigger.

BOOM! The shot echoed off the walls like cannon fire. She fired twice, hot brass casings bouncing off the partition's wall. Acrid powder fumes bit her nostrils. Then, three more shots. McFadden stood behind her, eying her technique. Reggie emptied the magazine at the target. Safety on, she put the pistol down, its muzzle pointed downrange.

McFadden hit the carrier toggle switch on the partition separating her lane from the next. The paper target flew to them. He beamed, giving her a thumbs-up. Five of her hits were center mass, four in the shoulder region, and three in the forehead. Three shots had pulled low and left. She draped the earmuffs around her neck and stepped back, arms crossed. "Satisfied?"

"Haven't lost your touch," he said.

"That's your kind way of saying I was anticipating the shot and pulling the trigger instead of squeezing it on the last three."

He shrugged. "All of 'em hit the paper, though."

McFadden smoothed pieces of masking tape over the holes in the target and sent it back downrange. After inserting a second magazine, he braced himself in a combat stance, the Beretta held out in front, shoulder high. He emptied the magazine in a steady volume of fire. Laying down the empty weapon, he brought the target back—all fifteen rounds tightly grouped, center mass.

"Show off," she said.

McFadden repaired the target with tape and sent it back. Reggie repeated her success with all hits center target, no misses. Grinning, McFadden pumped his fist.

"Practice makes perfect." He offered the last magazine but she declined.

McFadden loaded the Beretta and duplicated his first attempt, this time grouping his hits in the target's outlined head. He released the magazine and placed the empty Beretta in the clear plastic box along with the magazines. He dated the target and rolled it up for keeping. They backtracked, passing the husband-wife team shooting pistols under the watchful eye of their instructor. McFadden and Reggie went out through the soundproofed doors. He left the box on the counter.

"Thanks for the session, Sam. Am I good enough to go home early?"

Arms around her, he said, "You were terrific. My own Annie Oakley. You're a natural, Reggie. I pity the burglar who picks our house."

"Must be the personal instruction I get as the owner's wife. I'm heading home. Don't be late."

"Wouldn't miss it for the world."

They kissed and he sent her on her way. He had a gun range to run, after all.

Chapter 6

Ninoy Aquino International Airport, Manila

A sea of people surged through the main terminal, flooding the polished floors in waves of hurrying businessmen, tourists, and families with bawling infants. Scrums formed at baggage claim carousels, gates, and clogged escalators. Trailing their wheeled luggage, imperious, uniformed flight crews from thirty different airlines swam against the tide to reach their departure gates. A numbing cacophony of one hundred languages never ceased. A chaos of sorts ruled among the queues at duty-free shops, bars, and corridors leading to gates. Electric carts filled with the privileged and their luggage purred, parting the masses before them like yachts.

In the midst of the bedlam, Sparrow—one of 359 Hawaii-bound passengers—played the perfect chameleon. Wearing a black silk shirt, plain brown suit, a new shorter haircut, and a pair of stage glasses, he became an anonymous cipher, one not likely to be singled out for a chat by strolling airport security. To blend in further, he offered to help a young woman shepherding a pair of shuffling tortoise-like elders. The trio was boarding early and the couple's chaperon welcomed his assistance. His kindness earned him a thank you and a lower profile among the press of families, businessmen, and tourists queuing for the Sunday flight.

Once seated, Sparrow plugged in earphones and buried his nose in a Manila tabloid. Save for exchanging pleasantries with a flight attendant, he spoke to no one during the entire ten-hour flight. He dozed on and off.

At Honolulu's airport, he was low-key and compliant, drawing no attention through immigration and customs. He was asked a few cursory questions, his one piece of checked luggage given the briefest of looks. Past those hurdles, he stopped at a money exchange and traded what pesos he carried for more dollars.

He phoned the number Mendoza's note told him to memorize. His call had been expected and the reply was terse: *Go to the airport's food court, get a table, and wait. You will be contacted in ten minutes.* Sparrow did as told. He bought an iced tea and sat scanning a discarded copy of the *Honolulu Advertiser*. In ten minutes, a nubile Filipina in pink tank top and shorts, drink in hand, cellphone at her ear, took the table next to him and babbled. Eventually, she locked eyes with him and got up, the phone to her ear.

"Follow me, not too close," she said in passing.

Sparrow started after her, a dozen steps behind.

She led him outside to the sidewalk and lingered at the curb, apart from a growing crowd of new arrivals waiting for promised rides. Sparrow closed his eyes, breathing fragrant humid air, his ears filled with chatter and traffic. He opened his eyes and stepped to one side, ignoring his contact as instructed. He searched buses, hotel vans, taxis, and private vehicles streaming in the oncoming traffic.

"There is a blue van coming," she said without looking at him. "It will stop just beyond us, to your right. Get in behind the driver and say to him, 'I want you to take me to my brother's house.'"

"I understand."

"Good. I'll be right behind you."

Sparrow stepped off the curb, holding his suitcase. He took two steps and looked at the approaching traffic. Frowning, he glanced at his watch, then the cars. He stepped back to the sidewalk and looked at his watch again.

"What are you doing?" she hissed.

"Behaving like others," he said.

A blue van slowed, drifted to the curb and stopped ten feet to his right. Sparrow walked to the van, opened the side door, tossed in his bag, and got behind the driver.

"I want you to take me to my brother's house."

He got a nod. The woman he had followed slipped in the front passenger's seat without saying a word. The van accelerated, joining a stream of cars and taxis exiting the airport to join traffic heading west on H-1. Sparrow stared at the faces in the passing cars and vans. Most were brown like his, with the occasional *puting*—

white one—at the wheel. Battling to keep his amazement to himself, Sparrow studied the clustered houses blanketing the lower green slopes of Oahu's Ko'olau Range. They drove in silence for twenty minutes, passing Pearl Harbor on their left and the darkened Aloha Stadium. Traffic thinned. A blurred wall of trees lined the highway—monkey pod, lychee, and the familiar palm and banyan among the homes catching his eye. In the distance, the Wai'anae Mountains floated like a purple silhouette, beyond it the sea and a sun beginning to set clouds on fire. A mesmerized Sparrow studied the houses, the roads, and the landscape.

Crowded, yes. But unlike Manila. And certainly not Tondo's claustrophobic hive. He thought about his lie to Mendoza. Not about the killings; that part was true enough. But about having visited America—a place he had never been. This was all new.

What does it matter? he told himself. *I'm here.*

The driver took the Moanalua Road exit. He doubled back in a series of turns through neighborhood streets crowded with two-story frame houses and delivered his passengers to a safe house on Pearl City's Kaulike Drive. A trip that would have taken hours in Manila's sclerotic traffic had taken only twenty minutes. The driver pulled under a covered carport and killed the engine and lights. The woman got out and opened Sparrow's door.

"This way."

She led him through a door at the head of the carport and up a flight of stairs. A lanky, shirtless Filipino got up from the couch where he had been watching a mixed martial arts fight with the sound muted.

"This is Benny," she said. "He'll take care of you while you're with us."

"Welcome," said the fight fan, visibly nervous in the woman's presence.

"Show him to his room, Benny," she snapped.

"Sure. Down the hall, *manong*. At the end. You'll have it to yourself."

Benny started down the hall. His charge followed. The woman called after him. "You have forty-eight hours to rest. Don't go outside in daylight hours while you're here. Neighbors. They talk. Tomorrow afternoon I return with your new papers. Anything you need, ask Benny."

"Thank you."

"Hey, *manong*, you hungry?" said Benny.

"No." He shook his head. "Tired."

"Of course. You have your own comfort room. The rest of us have to share." He arched an eyebrow. "Gee but, you must be important, eh?"

Sparrow smiled and opened his suitcase to lay a few toiletries on the bed. "Wake me at noon."

"Noon? Okay. Whatever you say."

Sparrow's eyes ushered the man out of the room. He shut the door and stripped to his shorts. The room was sparsely furnished: a sagging double bed, a small wooden dresser, a smoky mirror, and a straight-backed, caned chair. A cheap garish floral print in a cheaper frame hung on one wall. The bathroom was simple: stool, sink, and tiled shower. Sparrow locked the door, took a quick shower, toweled dry, and brushed his teeth. He flipped the switch for a ceiling fan, dialed it to low, and lay down on the bed. In minutes, he was asleep.

Chapter 7

Kearny Office Park, San Diego

Silence filled a dead-end alley strewn with trash, the ideal site for an urban ambush. The head of the alley was a shuttered aluminum garage door, battered and spray-painted with ugly graffiti. One side of the alley was a ten-foot-high brick wall pocked with bullet holes. The opposite side was a rising facade with an abandoned street-level storefront scarred by fire and recently looted. The store's gaping display windows were shadowed by a balcony running the width of the two-story ruin—the perfect spot for a sniper. Commanding every approach, the balcony was the key.

Sam McFadden was feeling vulnerable. Having backed into the bottom of a narrow stairwell connected to the balcony, he gambled the sniper had not seen him take cover. McFadden had already lost four of his team to this same shooter, some of them SWAT team members. Whoever this guy was, he was good.

McFadden's calf muscles cramped. His back ached. He felt ancient. Off to his left somewhere, close friend and former Navy SEAL Tom Wolf faced his own problems. The two were the only survivors of what had been a six-man team. Time and ammo were running out.

The sniper would either show himself to draw McFadden's fire or Wolf would charge into the open as a decoy. It would be just like Wolf to sacrifice himself so McFadden could get in a shot.

Don't do it, Wolfman.

McFadden checked his remaining ammo. Six shots. Not enough to spray the balcony with covering fire once he gained the stairs. Slowing his breathing, McFadden heard someone moving toward him on his left.

Was it Wolf, or had the shooter left his perch and doubled back?

The sound got louder. McFadden leveled his weapon at the corner. A gloved hand popped into view and waved. McFadden lowered his weapon as Wolf crabbed into the stairwell. "Man, I'm glad to see you," whispered McFadden.

Wolf was grim. "We're the only two left."

"Don't I know it."

McFadden poked his weapon's muzzle at the stairs. "He's there. Cornered."

Wolf eyed the steps leading to the balcony and shook his head. "It's suicide to take those stairs."

"We don't have the luxury of waiting him out," hissed McFadden.

"Roger that. I have an idea."

"I'm all ears."

Wolf pointed to the low wall in the courtyard below the shooter's perch. "I'll crawl out there under cover and take him out when he shows."

Beads of perspiration streaked the grime on McFadden's face. "How we gonna flush him so we can get a shot?"

Wolf grinned. "You, my friend, will take the stairs when I signal you. He has to come out shooting. That's when I'll drop him."

"You said it was suicide to rush the stairs."

"So I did. We've got no choice. It's the best way to take him out. You might get lucky and get in a shot, Sam."

"Okay," said McFadden. "I'll go up when you signal. How much ammo you got left?"

Wolf checked his weapon. "Four rounds."

"Okay. My six will have to do. Get moving. I'll wait for your signal."

Wolf began crawling. He stopped, looked back over his shoulder. "Besides, I'm the better shot, Sam. You flush him and I'll drop him."

"Better shot my ass. If anything, we're equal."

Wolf inched forward, whispering behind him. "SEALs never miss, Sam."

"Bullshit."

Weapon cradled in his arms, Wolf slithered through piled trash, drawing fire from the balcony. Two rounds passed inches above his helmet, splattering the brick wall behind.

That was close, thought McFadden as he watched. He rose in a crouch, his weapon's muzzle aimed at the landing above, his eyes on Wolf.

Showtime.

A wave from Wolf and McFadden took the stairs, boots pounding the treads, warning the shooter he was coming.

McFadden rounded the corner at the landing and dropped to his knees, his finger on the trigger. The sniper flew out a doorway in a low crouch, firing his weapon point-blank. McFadden took a half-dozen shots in his torso and arms and tumbled backwards without firing a shot.

Wolf rose and fired. All four rounds hit the sniper. The man slumped against the balcony railings.

Silence. Then, Wolf raised both arms in triumph. "IT'S OVER!"

Lights flooded the scene like daylight. Applause filled the air along with whoops and laughter. Wolf removed his helmet and yelled up to a stunned McFadden, still on his back on the narrow balcony. Back on his feet, the sniper, a SWAT team member from the San Diego Police Department, offered a helping hand to McFadden. Both men leaned over the railing, looking down at a grinning Tom Wolf.

McFadden followed the shooter down the stairs and joined a jubilant Wolf in the middle of a crowd of civilians, military, and law enforcement, most wearing overalls splattered with rainbow-colored paint.

McFadden bumped fists with Wolf.

"It worked, Wolfman."

"Damn right it did. Tactics, Sam. SEAL tactics."

The vanquished sniper, bright yellow paint smeared across his chest protector, took off his helmet. Jabbing a gloved finger at Wolf, he said, "Location, location, location. I had you and Sam dead to rights, but you played it perfectly."

"Good old Sam," said Wolf. "He sacrificed himself for the cause."

McFadden waved his paintball gun weapon and called for quiet. "Okay, folks, dump your gear in the bins—weapons in the first one, overalls next to it, helmets and protective gear in the last one. Leave everything behind. Thanks for helping us inaugurate our new paintball maze. Now for pizza and cold beer. On the house!"

Cheers erupted in the cavernous warehouse space McFadden's contractor had transformed into an urban paintball shooting gallery. Connected to the indoor range and classrooms, the new space would double for laser tag, a tamer version of today's faux combat. McFadden had reason to be satisfied. The evening's inaugural tournament was the culmination of an eight-month construction project doubling his company's space.

McFadden spotted his wife—Reggie—and two of his team members' wives handing out plates with hot gourmet pizza. He and Wolf added their overalls and helmets to the growing pile. Two of McFadden's employees were collecting paintball guns, helmets, goggles, and protective vests for cleaning. Picnic tables for the paintball launch party had been set up in a corner by catering crews. McFadden embraced his wife and kissed her, leaving a smudge of pink paint on one cheek.

"Boys and their toys," she scolded above the din. "Are you happy with the opening festivities?"

McFadden grabbed a plate with pizza and offered Wolf one, along with a chilled beer. "Couldn't be happier. Here's to tonight's hero. The unscathed man of the hour, Tom Wolf."

More cheers from the crowd. Wolf raised his bottle in a toast.

"Here's to Sam and his partners. Long may their business prosper. And may all their villains suffer the same fate as our elusive shooter!"

A chorus of "Hear, Hear."

Wolf couldn't resist. "How are the knees, Sam?"

McFadden groaned. "Could you tell?"

"You were moving like an old man out there."

"I am an old man, Wolfman."

Wolf took a long swallow of cold beer. "Hell, Sam, just north of forty's not old. It's only a state of mind."

"In my case it was matter over mind. This is tougher than it looks."

"Agreed. It's a young man's game. But I have to say, you played your hand well today." Along with a squad of Marines, participants in the battle, Wolf crowed, "What can I tell you, Sam. There's no such thing as an old SEAL."

Reggie couldn't resist. "Peter Pan is what you meant to say."

The crowd roared its approval. Wolf frowned, then broke into laughter.

Sam McFadden may have been today's host but Tom Wolf was the star. As the lone survivor of the paintball battle, he was sought after by the town's media. Two local television reporters who had participated in the contest set up live shots with paint-splattered walls as a backdrop. One TV crew questioned McFadden about his decision to build an urban paintball maze. A petite, tanned blonde from KSWB, the Fox affiliate, corralled a grinning Tom Wolf once he finished with a reporter from the *Union-Tribune.*

Wolf was good copy. Towering over the buxom mike-wielding reporter, he replayed the combat for her by using empty beer bottles on a tabletop. He multi-tasked—explaining urban warfare tactics while brazenly flirting. Other players, still wearing overalls smeared with paintball hits, mugged from the sidelines, hooting at his on-camera answers. It was all in good fun. When the crowds thinned, Wolf had his fifteen minutes of fame, the blonde's cellphone number, and a Friday night dinner date.

Having witnessed the exchange, Reggie scolded him. "You're incorrigible."

"I am that," said Wolf, busy helping caterers drain ice from coolers.

McFadden said, "I had a hard time keeping a straight face during my interview while you were next door working hard to impress that reporter."

"Just trying to lighten up your image, Sam. I wanted her to know you have a fun side, that you're not just all business."

Reggie linked arms with McFadden and shook her head at Wolf. "I saw it all. You were shameless."

Wolf tossed a bag of ice to one of the caterers. "Well, which is it, Reggie? I thought you said I was incorrigible. Am I shameless as well?"

She laughed. "Both."

"Guilty," said Wolf.

Chapter 8

Lindbergh Field, San Diego, two days later

Sparrow arrived on the mainland after an afternoon flight from Honolulu. Rechristened as Ramon Reyes—the California driver's license and Social Security card he carried proved it—Mendoza's contacts in Hawaii had done their job well. Traveling on a domestic flight bypassed the risk of immigration and customs. A pretty boy, wearing a greasy pompadour, mirrored sunglasses, and an open-necked floral shirt, paced at the bottom of the escalator in terminal two. The gangbanger caricature held a cardboard sign labeled "Welcome, Mr. Reyes" in large black marker. If Sparrow had hoped to arrive incognito, the clown with his sign had ruined the attempt.

He stepped off the moving stairs without making eye contact with this San Diego one-man welcoming committee. His flight's fellow passengers ringed the baggage carousel, which began to rumble, coughing up luggage. Sparrow plucked his bag and walked up behind the man with the sign on the edge of the crowd.

"Where's your car?"

The greeter turned in surprise. "Mr. Reyes?"

"Get rid of the sign," Sparrow hissed, "and take me to your car."

"Right outside." He reached for the bag. "If you will follow..."

Sparrow was already on the move, suitcase in hand.

His hapless host tossed the cardboard sign in a trash can and hustled outside, pointing to a black Escalade. Sparrow beat him to it, tossed his bag on the back seat, and shut the door. A bullet-headed Filipino at the wheel glanced nervously in the rearview mirror at his passenger.

The man with the pompadour and shades slid next to the driver. "You'll like San Diego," he said to Sparrow. "We have a world-class zoo, beaches—"

"We can drop the pretense. I am no tourist. Just drive."

"My orders were to—"

"I know what your orders say. I'm here. Take me to wherever you're supposed to deliver me. I'm hungry and tired."

The driver glanced at the man in the passenger seat and shrugged.

The pompadour's owner began, "I have to be sure—"

Sparrow cut him off with a wave. "Go. We sort this out later."

"This is most unusual."

"Consider me welcomed. You want me to tell the man who sent me that I spent my first hour in America arguing with amateurs?"

Silenced by the outburst, the pouting host signaled the chauffeur to do as ordered. They left the airport, crowded marinas, and waterfront with its tourists behind. Sparrow sat back, the downtown a blur of high-rises and sleek office buildings. They headed north on a highway of bumper-to-bumper traffic.

From the backseat: "You have a name?"

"Manny."

"Where are we going, Manny?"

"Mira Mesa. Not far."

"My instructions say you have a place prepared."

"Yes, a safe house."

"I will want privacy."

"You will have it."

"Good."

"You want a woman?"

Sparrow sighed. "Do I look like I need a woman, Manny?"

"Uh, I just thought. Maybe—"

"I'm here to do one thing, Manny."

"Of course. Maybe the woman later, eh?"

Fool. Sparrow sank back against the seat, fingers massaging his temple. *I was told the gangs here were professionals who inspired fear in their rivals. Surely I'm not expected to work with this idiot.*

He finished the ride in silence.

Chapter 9

San Diego Police Department Headquarters

Detective Mike McManus, an auburn-haired fourth-generation Irish cop with a broad, freckled face, was on his third cup of coffee, a setback in a two-week battle to wean himself from caffeine. His partner, Bob Mathis, a square-faced methodical investigator fond of spreadsheets, poked his head in McManus's office doorway.

"Bagged your battle with coffee?"

McManus shrugged. "Busted. Gave it a try. What can I say?"

"Not an easy habit to break, Mike."

"Don't make excuses for me."

Mathis took a seat in front of the desk, one of his charts in hand. "Tomorrow's a fresh start."

McManus drained his coffee and crumpled the paper cup into a ball. "So, what's the latest on that rumor gangbangers were meeting a VIP at the airport?"

Mathis slouched in the chair. "It's true. Our boys are up to no good as usual."

McManus lofted the crushed coffee cup at a corner wastebasket and missed. "So who's our big shot?"

"Don't know. Came in on the five o'clock from Honolulu."

"You might wanna get Rodriguez in on this. He knows all the players."

Mathis folded his sheet in crisp quarters and pocketed it. "He's in LA until the end of the week for that gang workshop the feds are running."

"Right. Let's bring him up to speed first thing when he gets back."

"Will do."

"Any video of this guy?"

"I've got a call in to the Harbor PD asking about it. Won't be a problem to get it. If we're lucky they got a face shot."

McManus got up, stretched, and did a few quick knee bends behind his desk to take his mind off coffee. "Do we know who met this guy?"

Mathis plucked a notebook from his back pocket. "One of our guys was working a dog at the airport. He ID'd Biggy Pacheco behind the wheel of the pickup car."

"Biggie, huh? Do we know who else played welcoming committee?"

Mathis shrugged. "He didn't know the guy. Have to wait for the video."

"Okay, let's make sure we follow up. I don't like it. Some out-of-towner arrives and gets a ride with some of our local scumbags."

"Roger that."

McManus stood, stretched both arms above his head to loosen up. "Changing subjects. How you coming with that whack job at the fitness club?"

"My stalker? He's got himself a lawyer now. Won't talk. But he's pissing in the wind if he thinks we're gonna cut him loose. We got a search warrant for his computer. Randall's betting we'll have an email trail a mile long."

"Good work. These numbnuts never seem to learn."

"Which guarantees us job security."

McManus snorted. "Always the optimist, huh, Bob?"

Mathis followed his partner into the hallway where the two carried their conversation down a stairwell, McManus saying, "Let me know ASAP when you hear about any airport video. I don't like the idea of some mystery man showing up in our town and getting a ride with our bad boys."

"You're repeating yourself, Mike. Maybe your sixth sense at work?"

"Something like that," said McManus. "Or maybe the caffeine."

"We'll have something after lunch," said Mathis. "I'll keep you posted."

McManus paused. "Do that."

Mid-afternoon, Mathis intercepted McManus in the headquarters parking lot. "You must be living right."

"You got something for me, right?"

Mathis held up a disc. "Affirmative. Harbor PD copied us video of that VIP Biggy Pacheco picked up yesterday at the airport."

"We get a face?"

"Face and a name."

"Outstanding. So give it up."

Mathis pocketed the disc and scanned his notebook. "Ramon Reyes. It matched the cardboard sign that low-life was holding up to welcome him."

"So we got a match. Likely as not it's an alias. You running Reyes through the system?"

"As we speak."

"It's worth a try. We could get lucky, but I wouldn't bet on it."

"I'll follow it as far as it goes."

"Do that." McManus held the door for Mathis and followed
him inside. "Good work, Bob. Let's check out the video. Get
one of the gang guys in to take a look."

The two went upstairs to McManus's office and popped
the DVD in his computer. While McManus watched the
screen, Mathis called in one of the street gang officers.

The three viewed the looped video but came up blank on
the visitor's face. The fifteen-second clip showed a lesser-
known gang member posing with a handmade sign at the
bottom of the terminal's escalator. The three laughed.

"Look at that idiot," said McManus. "He probably
thought he was going to impress his guest with a sign. Can
you believe these guys?"

"At least we have a name," said Mathis.

"Reyes. Probably an alias," said the gang cop. "Worth
checking though."

McManus said, "That's what we think. Just make sure
you pass the word," said McManus. "Have your guys stop
by to look at the video when they have a minute, will ya?
Somebody might recognize this guy."

The cop nodded and left.

"Could be nothing," said Mathis, replaying the clip.
"Or, could be something about to go down. Maybe some
pro muscle from out of town for a sit down."

"Or somebody just passing through."

"Possibly," said McManus. "We could always haul Biggie
Pacheco in."

"Waste of time. Nothing illegal here. Biggie's a rock.
He'd never roll over."

McManus paused the video, pointed to the clownish
figure in the mirrored shades holding the welcoming sign.
"Here's our key. Let's ID this tour guide and bring him in
for a chat. Maybe we can find out where they took our
mystery man."

Chapter 10

Mira Mesa

Sparrow came out on the covered lanai with his tea and sat in the dying sun beside Manny Ramos, his inept greeter. In the privacy of the home's walled back yard, the SUV's driver, Biggy Pacheco, and a beautiful, barefooted, pony-tailed Filipina dressed in white dueled in the lengthening shadows. The couple sparred with *yantoks*—pairs of supple rattan canes used in *eskrima*—one of the Philippines's signature martial arts disciplines. The hulking chauffeur and the slender porcelain-skinned woman—an odd match to the untrained eye—parried each other's blows in a choreographed *pas de deux*.

Sparrow was intrigued by the match. "Who is she?" he asked.

"This her auntie's house, *manong*. She work with us."

"I know that, *payaso*—I mean her name."

"Ah. Tala. It means—"

"Bright star," he interrupted, his eyes on the woman.

"Of course. I forget, eh."

"She is very good. Very fast."

"Biggie has his hands full, I think. She can kick ass, *manong*."

"She's beautiful," said Sparrow. "Skillful in the way she moves."

"And deadly. You thinking of bedding her, think again."

"She prefers girls?"

"Hey, she not like that. But Tala does the bedding, not the man."

"Why would you think I am considering such a thing?"

Ramos shook his head as if the question was not worth answering.

Sparrow's eyes never left the woman as the combat escalated. Back and forth the pair went, the woman feinting, then striking home. Pacheco defending, backpedaling, the rhythmic sound of clattering sticks filling the air. The woman pressed the attack, backing her opponent into a corner, raining a blur of lightning-fast blows. Pacheco cried out, halting the contest.

Sparrow and Ramos applauded from their perch.

The victor flashed an irritated look their way, brushed past them without a word, and went into the house, shutting the sliding glass door behind her.

Manny Ramos bayed at the defeated chauffeur. "Hey, Biggie, what happen? You give up too easy, eh?"

"You like try?"

"No way, *manong*. I see the way she treat you, eh."

"Tell our guest how she beat you like a dog, Manny. No shame. She's too good, eh." Sweating profusely, Pacheco tossed the *yantoks* on the lanai and went over to the garden hose tap. He stripped off his sweatshirt, doused his head and torso, then rubbed his body with a towel. "Not hard to figure out. You don't fight Tala, she don't respect you. Simple as that." He threw the towel at Ramos and looked at Sparrow.

"You know how to fight? Maybe you challenge her, eh?"

"I do some training before," he said. "I have other things on my mind now." Ramos giggled. "Oh, yeah. Other things. I think he likes her."

Sparrow plucked a cane and prodded Ramos. "You talk like a fool."

Pacheco said, "You have my permission to use it on him."

"I don't need permission, *manong*. But lucky for him, I save my energy."

The driver, sweatshirt around his neck, paused at the sliding doors. "Okay, save your energy. I think you'll have to challenge Tala if you expect her to work with you."

"Fair enough. I need her help. Maybe before the week is out if she is willing."

Pacheco roared. "Oh, she willing, *manong*. She like to fight."

"Good," said Sparrow, "so do I. Now, about the gun I am to be given."

"In your hands tomorrow."

"Good."

Chapter 11

"Hell, old man. Nam was a picnic compared to Afghanistan."

A graying, ponytailed, tattooed biker, wearing a sleeveless leather vest decorated with a painted dragon and a Marine helicopter squadron's Vietnam in-country dates, was ten minutes into an escalating argument with a younger loudmouth. The graying hog owner offered up an apology of sorts.

"You had to be there, pal. Wasn't no picnic. Now, I ain't saying Afghanistan was a cakewalk…"

The overture was ignored. "You saying we had it easy, asshole?"

Wolf cocked his head to one side, listening to the confrontation at the nearby bar. He and Crystal Hamm, the blond reporter from the Fox affiliate who had covered the opening of McFadden's paintball gallery, nursed drinks while waiting for a booth to open. The restaurant, a local secret with excellent cuisine, was one of Wolf's favorites when in town. He had taken all his dates here, promising great seafood, wine, and romantic candlelight. The furnishings, a funky mix of brass nautical gear, nets, and dark walls of weathered planking, were just the right mix of tacky décor and ambiance. The evening had been mellow until this moment.

As Wolf settled on the high stool opposite Crystal, he tried to ignore the rising voices from the bar. He said, "I'm glad you got the assignment to cover Sam McFadden's open house."

Crystal, who had caught part of the bar's mounting argument, turned back to Wolf. "Me too. I've heard about paintball tournaments but never thought I'd cover one, let alone take part."

"You look good covered in yellow paint. It becomes you."

"Flatterer."

"No, I'm serious. You handled yourself well for—"

"A girl?"

"Not going there," said Wolf, hands raised in surrender. "I meant to say you handled yourself well for a media person with no combat experience."

She scoffed at the compliment. "Ha, as if you didn't notice. I lasted all of five minutes before I was covered in paint. I let my team down."

"It's the thought that counts," said Wolf. "At least you were game."

She sipped her drink and said, "I'm curious. What's your connection to Sam McFadden?"

Wolf rubbed his chin, smiling at a memory. "We both served in the Philippines. Mindanao. Southernmost island. Sam had retired to Zamboanga to fulfill his dream of a live-aboard dive boat, a converted trawler. I threw in some money as well and joined him when I left the service."

"Partners?"

"Yep. Seemed like a good idea at the time. Sam got mixed up with some Filipino general's daughter. Saved her life, actually. We stepped on some toes. Bad actors. Gangsters.

Ended up in a fight for Sam's dream and our lives. Lost some friends in the process."

She put a hand on his arm. "Sorry to hear that. What happened to the boat?"

"The general got it. He was a crook, and not the only one. It was a mess."

"Lose your shirts?"

"We got out okay, actually. He married the girl and landed on his feet here."

"And you?"

"I found a spot in Washington. Did some contracting. Kicked around."

"So, you haven't grown up yet, huh?"

"Something like that," Wolf said. "And what about you, Miss Fox News?"

Her answer was drowned out by rising voices. Wolf, irritated at the interruption, stared at the crowded bar. The evening's chief antagonist, a beefy, bearded, bandana-wearing barfly in denim repeated his claim, his voice rising.

"You're telling me Afghanistan was fucking easy?"

The biker backed up. "Didn't say that. What I'm saying is..."

The big man and two companions edged closer to the mustachioed biker, their combined bulk dwarfing him. Whiskey-powered bravado mixed with testosterone was a volatile mix. Wolf had seen it countless times before, had been in the trio's shoes in his younger days when goaded by brawling friends in a dozen bars.

He and Crystal stopped talking to watch the contest taking place just feet from their perch. The red-faced alpha male glowered at the biker. "You ain't saying shit, old man. You're talking out your ass like you don't know nothing. Iraq was hell."

"I thought you said Afghanistan."

An embarrassed pause. "Don't fuck with me, old-timer."

The senior, smoldering, turned away, focusing on his drink. The biker's woman, a chesty over-ripe redhead wearing jeans and leather chaps, but still a looker, defended her man. "Hey, lay off, we're all family here."

"I don't see no family here, only a shit-for-brains senior citizen," snarled the bully. His friends howled at the joke. A nearby bartender, just a slip of a girl, busied herself with other customers to stay out of the line of fire.

"Assholes," murmured the redhead under her breath.

Wolf and Crystal watched the action in the bar's wide mirror. He thought about taking their drinks and ushering her to the dining room, but the antagonists were blocking access. That, and he was curious how the confrontation was going to play out.

"Wha'd you say, bitch?" sneered the trio's leader.

The biker turned to the bigger man. "Ain't no call to talk to her like that."

"Says who?"

A deadly silence between the two camps. Wolf, wary of where this was going, slid off his stool between Crystal and the would-be combatants as a precaution. He kept his expression neutral.

The redhead stepped in the gap, pleading eyes on her man, a hand on his arm. "C'mon, Walt, we don't need this. Let's go."

Fight or flight, thought Wolf. *What's it going to be?*

The beard was pushing his luck, mimicking in falsetto, "Yeah, let's go, Walt. Better listen to your old lady. Got to get your wrinkled ass back to assisted living before they lock the doors for the night."

More drunken laughter from the three men.

"Take it outside, folks."

The bar's owner, a muscular, barrel-shaped peacekeeper miraculously appeared. He planted thick arms on the polished mahogany. "What's it gonna be?"

The biker, seething with indignation, abandoned the bar to the three drunks and moved sideways to the restaurant's entryway. Wolf imagined the man's rage at his impotence. The menacing trio ignored the watching bar owner and the retreating couple. They turned their attention in Wolf's direction.

"What are you looking at?"

Wolf shook his head. "Nothing. We were just about to leave."

"Outside, gentlemen." The owner, cellphone in hand, repeated his warning. "I don't want any trouble in my place."

"We're leaving," said Wolf, backing up, his arm at Crystal's elbow.

"A wise choice," said the bully's second, thumbing at his leader. "You don't want to mess with a Navy SEAL."

Wolf paused. "Oh? Navy SEAL, huh? You guys are tough, I hear."

"Tom, don't toy with this Neanderthal," said Crystal under her breath.

The biker and his woman, mesmerized by what was unfolding, stood in the entry, unable to move. Ignoring them, the trio's leader focused on Wolf, his new target. "What are you, a wiseass?"

"Not at all," said Wolf. "I respect the SEALs' reputation, that's all."

The bearded bully locked on Crystal Hamm, his eyes undressing her, a carnivorous grin spreading. Wolf knew the look.

"Hey, I know you," said the drunk. "You're that hot babe on TV."

Wolf stepped in front of the offender. Nodding at the door, he said. "You've obviously had a lot to drink, friend. Maybe now would be a good time for you and your buddies to leave...you know, while you still can."

Wolf's challenger held up his hands in surrender, a mocking smile spreading.

"Oh, we should be scared shitless, boys. Suddenly our friend here grows a pair." He turned to his laughing friends, clumsily telegraphing the coming punch.

Wolf readied for the blow.

The big man whirled, his fist aiming for Wolf's head. Ducking inside the blow, Wolf drove his right knee deep in the man's groin while simultaneously grasping his attacker's right wrist, twisting it.

The stunned man fell to his knees, writhing in pain.

A second attacker leaped at Wolf but was brought down by the biker who aimed a booted mule kick at the man's knee, crippling the joint. The man collapsed, howling. The third man, collared by the bartender wielding a sawed-off bat overhead, surrendered without a fight. The melee had lasted all of six seconds.

Transfixed diners, who had witnessed the entire fight from argument to finish, rose from their seats in thunderous, prolonged applause.

"Outside," bellowed the bar's owner, prodding the only untouched member of the offending trio. The redhead opened the door. Wolf, the biker, and the bar owner dragged the attackers outside just as two patrol cars arrived.

Chapter 12

In the parking lot, Wolf and Crystal gave their statements to officers, along with those of the biker and his woman. The bar's owner, plus a crowd of eager witnesses from the dining room, corroborated Wolf's version. The two brawlers, *hors de combat*, were treated by a team of EMTs and placed in the back seat of one patrol car. The untouched member of the threesome was cuffed and driven away in a second car.

After good-natured banter with the bar's owner, Wolf walked Crystal across the asphalt to where the biker straddled his Harley. The redhead was in an animated conversation with her pony-tailed man.

Wolf saw Crystal to his car. "Give me a minute," he said.

"Are you planning an encore?"

"Just want to have a word with this guy and his lady."

"You've done enough for one evening. Don't do anything stupid."

"Wouldn't think of it. Be right back."

She locked the doors behind him and Wolf walked to the Harley.

"You had my back, friend," he said.

The woman flashed a relieved smile at Wolf. "That's my Walt. I knew he wasn't gonna walk away."

Wolf nodded at the redhead. "Good thing he stuck around, ma'am. Three to one odds is never a good number."

"Hell, in my day I coulda taken those guys, you know."

Wolf smiled. "Hey, I believe you. But that was then, this is now. Once something like this gets going you never know where it will end. For all we knew, those guys coulda been packing. Not like they gave us a choice."

The woman spat her words. "The world is full of assholes and we had to run into three of them tonight. C'mon, Walt, let's go home."

The biker stood on the pegs and kicked his hog into life. "Glad you were there," he shouted. "Karma, man."

"Call it what you want," said Wolf. "You handled yourself well."

The biker's lady climbed aboard the idling motorcycle. "I wanted to leave but he hates to back down, you know."

Wolf said, "I figured as much. So do I." He held out his hand. "Tom Wolf."

The biker took Wolf's hand. "Walt Jonski."

"I'm Sarah," said the redhead.

Wolf eyed the hog owner's jacket art. "Vietnam, huh?"

Jonski's wife said, "Walt was a crew chief on H-34s."

The Harley idled in a muscular rumble. Jonski said, "We affectionately called 'em Dogs. Two tours, back to back with the Flying Tigers—HMM-361."

"I know the feeling."

"Hell, you're too young to have been in Nam."

"True. Different era, but I got around."

"Iraq? Afghanistan?"

"That and a few other stops along the way."

"What branch?"

"Navy. Special Ops."

A puzzled look, then a light in the eyes. "SEALs?"

Wolf nodded.

"That why you took on that guy? He said he was a SEAL, you know."

Shaking his head, Wolf said, "I seriously doubt he was the real deal."

The biker laughed. "Hell, we whipped their asses didn't we?"

"Yeah, but your lady's right. Sometimes it's better to walk away."

Jonski put the bike in gear, revved the engine. "Not tonight, brother." He handed Wolf a business card. "We have a reunion group from the squadron. Bikers like me. Old but ornery. Call me if you ever need backup."

Smiling at Jonski's bravado, Wolf read and pocketed the card.

Wolf backed up and waved. "Semper Fi, Walt."

"Semper Fi."

The Harley roared away, the redhead turning to blow a kiss at Wolf. He grinned and crossed the parking lot to his car. He tapped on the window and Crystal popped the locks.

"Wasn't sure if I should open the door," she said.

"Sorry our evening's ruined."

She reached across the seat and tousled Wolf's hair, purring, "Who said it's ruined...or that it's over?"

Chapter 13

Sparrow rose early and waited for Tala to appear on the lanai. They acknowledged each other with polite nods. He sat at the table opposite her, sipping green tea in the latticework's shade. Spooning a bowl of yogurt, a martial arts magazine in her other hand, she ignored him. She continued reading until he broke the silence.

"I will need your help," he said.

She put down her spoon and magazine. "Really? My auntie said we were only to provide you a safe place until you've completed your job."

"True. But I find myself at a disadvantage in your city."

She resumed reading.

He put down the cup and cleared his throat. "I was told your people would assist me in whatever way they could."

Tala lowered the magazine and raised an eyebrow. "That is not my concern.

You have shelter. You have privacy. You have a car if you need one. You take your meals here." She paused. "And you have the gun Biggie promised."

"Are there no secrets here?"

"I saw the exchange. There must be no violence in this house. You are a guest in my auntie's home, remember that."

"And I am most grateful to your aunt for providing shelter."

"What are you asking, then?"

Sparrow picked up the teacup in both hands, his eyes on the beautiful woman.

"I need to find a man, my employer's enemy."

"And why do you seek this man?"

He shrugged. "That is not your concern. I only need find him."

Her eyes narrowed. "Are you to eliminate this man?"

"Perhaps."

"You want my help? Perhaps you will put me at risk. Tell me why."

"It could be dangerous."

"Ah, you have come here to kill a man. Why not admit this?"

"I cannot trust just anyone."

She leaned forward, hands folded under her chin. "Of course not. But I'm curious. Why do you ask me?"

"As I said. I do not have the time to spend wandering in circles looking for this particular man."

"And for that you need my help?"

Sparrow risked a faint smile. "Yes. I believe I would be less conspicuous in your company for what I need to do."

She laughed, her perfect white teeth contrasting with light skin, her dark eyes intrigued. "Is this the best you can do?"

Sparrow sat back, puzzled by the rebuke. "What do you mean?"

"I've been watching you, Ramon Reyes, mystery guest. Sparrow, as you call yourself. I know you have been following my every movement. I feel your eyes on me. Don't deny it."

He reddened. "I admire your grace, that's all. Your skill at *eskrima* interests me, that's all.

"Liar."

He bristled. "I am not used to being spoken to like this."

She laughed despite his embarrassment. "No, I am sure you are shown much respect in the Philippines, *pinoy*. But you are not in Manila, Ramon Reyes, if that's really your name...or where you come from. This is America. Things are different here if you haven't noticed."

He fell silent, unsure how to reason with the bold woman in front of him. She casually threw an arm over the back of her chair and said, "Okay, so you say you need my assistance, yes?"

He nodded.

"I don't just drop everything and help you with whatever you need done."

"I don't expect you to," he said. "I have money."

"It's not always about money, though I'll take it." She stood, her hands planted on the table. "Just so we understand each other...You want my help. Earn it. You know how to fight? *Eskrima?*"

"I can try. You would be a worthy opponent."

"Well then, put up a good fight, *pinoy*. I don't give quarter."

"After watching you, I would not expect it."

"This evening. When it's cooler. I don't want to tire you out."

"As you wish. Does that mean you will help me?"

She threw back her head, laughing, her long black hair cascading over her shoulders. "You understand? If you win, yes, I help you. But I don't think you will win."

"And if we draw?"

"Even if you can win a draw, maybe I help you."

"Good. I'll be ready."

Her eyes hardened. "But I don't think you will gain a draw either."

"We'll see."

Snatching her magazine and bowl from the table, she headed inside, saying over her shoulder, "Just so you know, I will hurt you...not badly, but enough to make you regret your boast."

"Fair warning."

"And when I win, *pinoy*..."

"If you win."

"No, when I win...you will tell me who you really are."

He paused. "Then you leave me no choice. I have to win."

Chapter 14

That evening, Sparrow gambled on his quickness to Tala's aggressiveness. He needed to win the bout, or at least a draw. The contest was not part of the original plan, but marooned as he was, and with the clock running, he thought the duel might work to his advantage.

Ramos's chatty counsel was no help. "She come at you first thing, *manong*.

She press until you fall back. Once she get you in the corner, you done. Over. Fold up. Go to your knees quick."

"Is that what happened to you?"

"Hey, she get lucky, that's all."

"That's not how Biggie tells it."

While waiting for Tala to show, he did stretching exercises on the patio while Ramos babbled more inane advice. To his surprise, Biggie Pacheco arrived with a glowering older gangbanger he had invited to witness the bout. The stranger, street royalty of some sort, projected a malevolent presence. The man claimed the best of the patio chairs and waited for the contest to begin. Two more *pinoy* drifted in from the garage and exchanged handshakes with Pacheco. Money passed hands, another disturbing sign. What had begun as a private challenge by Tala in exchange for her help had taken on a life of its own.

Ignoring the newcomers, Sparrow sought a corner in the walled backyard. He closed his eyes and slowed his breathing, blocking out the scene. Murmuring from the onlookers caught his attention. He opened his eyes.

Tala, in loose white clothing, barefooted and unsmiling, her long hair tied back, stepped from the house, imperiously parting the spectators. Despite the reason for their meeting, Sparrow found it hard to ignore her beauty. She strode to the center of the yard and summoned Biggie Pacheco. The big man showed, *yantoks* under one arm. He beckoned to Sparrow. The combatants drew close and faced each other, their expressions neutral. Pacheco handed two reed canes to each.

Tala flexed her canes, theatrically cutting the air with precise blows, testing the weapons. Sparrow waited quietly until she finished. Her dark eyes caught his and she nodded. Each assumed a martial stance, a partial crouch, right leg forward, canes ready.

She struck first. Slashing left and right, she rained a flurry of blows at Sparrow. He parried, giving ground, matching her every move with defensive strikes of his own. Back and forth, the pair went, clattering canes rapping out a rhythm as if rehearsed. She tested him, beginning with a series of five angles of attack, then nine, then twelve. He met her every attempt by skillfully deflecting each blow. She cut at him with horizontal strikes and vertical thrusts. Sparrow sidestepped her attack and came at her with a rapid flurry of figure eights, then reversed the pattern. She backed away but he closed, increasing his tempo with vertical strokes, circular

cuts, diagonal sweeps and dazzling wrist moves with the
yantoks. Neither would yield. The staccato beat of the sticks
mesmerized their audience. Pacheco and the others sat in
rapt attention at the level of skill they were witnessing.

Slowly, methodically, Tala pressed Sparrow toward a
walled corner. But then he scored, delivering a stinging blow
to Tala's right cheekbone. A red welt appeared but she kept
pushing, bloodying knuckles on Sparrow's left hand.
Favoring his wounded hand, he retreated toward the corner,
giving ground. She pushed ahead, raining blows in one
continuous movement. Sparrow drew her in, stung her
forehead with two quick slaps of rattan, and then sidestepped
a series of repeated thrusts.

Summoning every ounce of strength, Tala, her fury
aroused, kept coming.

Sparrow's ability to evade her best moves enraged
her. Then, she was the one cornered. Sparrow delivered
a rapid series of low blows, scoring with painful hits to
her ankles, knees, and thighs. He increased the power of
his strikes, combining vertical blows with horizontal
ones, tapping her biceps at will, punishing her best
efforts to pierce his defenses. Her desperation only
increased as Sparrow moved in for the kill. She raised
both canes to ward off strikes at her head, leaving her
mid-section open. He jabbed her ribcage repeatedly,
inflicting crippling, stinging hits.

"Enough!" yelled Pacheco's guest. "Finish already!"

Sparrow stepped back, his eyes on a winded, defeated
Tala. She lowered her gaze, avoiding his stare. Nodding,
she raised her bruised right hand, the *yantok* slipping from
her grasp. Tala shuffled past him, eyes downcast, her
lower lip bloodied and swollen. She crossed the patio in
silence and went into the house without acknowledging the
hushed audience.

Pacheco collected cash from disgruntled bettors who had never seen Tala beaten. Among the losing gamblers was Pacheco's guest—sullen at the contest's outcome. Followed by fawning acolytes, he slipped out through the garage. The crowd broke up, clearing the patio. A cowed Manny Ramos, silent for once, brought a wet towel to Sparrow, exchanging it for the battered canes.

Waving a fistful of bills, Pacheco pushed Ramos aside and approached Sparrow. "Hey, *manong*, you make one helluva fight, eh? I gamble on you and you make me a rich man. I had a feeling, eh? Nevah seen anyone take Tala like that. You know how to fight, man."

"Tala. She going to be okay?"

Pacheco waved away the concern. "Ah, *walang problema* —no problem. She's tough. She'll look rough for a couple days, no matter. She got her ass beat. Gonna take time for her pride to heal, you know? No problem."

"She'll help me now, eh?"

Pacheco roared. "Help you? You earned it. Sure, she help you. She got to now. Give her a few days, *manong*. She be ready to do whatever you need."

Ramos chirped, "She'll make you coffee now. Anything you like."

"Shut up!" yelled Pacheco. "You want to say that to Tala's face?"

Sparrow glared at Ramos, who backed away.

"Biggie," sighed Sparrow, "I'm going to take a shower and sleep."

"Yeah, you look like you went ten rounds with Pac-Man himself."

"I feel like it."

"But you won, *manong*. That's the point, eh?"

"I had no choice."

Chapter 15

Biggie was right. It took only days for Tala to heal physically. But emotionally, she was withdrawn in defeat. Her haughty separation from the others sharing the home disappeared, replaced with a subdued version of her former self. She was correct, even formal in her interaction with Sparrow. Words were at a minimum. Having bested her at her game, Sparrow thought it best to play an aloof card to complete her humbling. He thought to give her at least seven days before he sought her promised help. His plan was to approach her at the beginning of the new week to find the man he had come to kill, but she waited only until mid-week to take the first step.

The third day dawned the same. Sparrow took tea on the patio to avoid Manny Ramos's bothersome chatter. Tala kept to herself. At noon, one of Biggie's runners, sent to forage for fast food, stopped by with bags of greasy fried chicken and biscuits. Sparrow longed for Filipino food but had been warned by Biggie to stay out of sight by avoiding local restaurants. He chafed at confinement. Somewhere out there was the man he had come to kill.

The day unspooled. Sparrow began to doubt whether his victory over Tala had been a tactical blunder. He ate little, took tea that evening, and retreated behind his closed door.

That night, he heard Tala outside his room, tapping on his door. He tensed, unsure of the reason for the visit. She slipped inside and closed the door behind her. Moonlight filtering through the blinds cast shadows across the floor. Turning his head to the left, his half-lidded eyes followed her as she approached. He sighed, as if in deep sleep. He felt her pause, inches from the edge of his mattress.

Sparrow lay on his right side, his back to her. Feigning sleep, he stirred as if dreaming, his hand gripping the butterfly knife under his pillow as a precaution.

Tala undid the belt and let her robe fall around her feet. Moonlight fell on her nakedness, highlighting her breasts and the curve of her hips. Slipping into his bed, she tugged the sheet to her chin and lay still. Sparrow turned to the wall, eyes open, his hand on the knife.

Tala shifted under the sheet, pressing her body against his back. She lifted her left arm and slid it around his waist, drawing closer, fitting her body to his. Sparrow let go of the knife.

"Are you awake?" she whispered.

Sparrow did not respond. Content to have her in his bed, he fell asleep, certain there would be other nights like this. His disciplined restraint would work in his favor.

I will do the bedding, not you, dear Tala, he thought. *It's better that way.*

In the morning, Sparrow awoke with her in his arms, their legs entangled. He kissed the sleeping Tala and slipped from the bed without waking her. He gazed at her naked body, then draped a sheet over her when she stirred. He went into the bathroom and closed the door. Sparrow showered, taking his time. When he toweled dry, he returned to find his bed empty. Sparrow dressed, made the bed, and went to the kitchen.

A grinning Biggie Pacheco rumbled by on his way to the carport. He nodded at Sparrow as if sharing a secret and then drove away. Manny Ramos climbed from the lower level, his disheveled hair and wrinkled clothes testimony to another sleepless night. Markedly more disagreeable than usual, he made a show of snubbing Sparrow to make coffee for himself. The two did not speak. Sparrow thought Tala's nocturnal visit the reason for the younger man's jealous pouting, but he ignored it. He made tea and took it outside in the cool morning air. He stayed there until the first warming rays burned off the night's dew from the grass carpet. The sliding glass doors behind him opened. Footsteps and the familiar perfume—Tala.

Sparrow looked up at Tala, hovering over him. He smiled. She returned the look, the night in his bed now a shared, erotic memory for both. He knew instantly his tactic of self-control had triumphed. Her next remark confirmed it.

"Tell me again who is this man you seek."

"His name is Samuel McFadden. I am here because those who sent me know he lives in this city."

"Give me a few minutes on my computer to find this man."

"I would be grateful."

She brushed her hand against the back of his neck. "Leave it to me." She left him alone with his tea and returned fifteen minutes later with a printout of McFadden's business and home addresses.

Impressed, Sparrow studied the sheet in his hands. "This business of his. Am I correct that McFadden runs a gun range? This is permitted here?"

Tala nodded. "It is."

"I was told he was a warrior, but this means he may be more dangerous than I thought."

"True. Perhaps you should think of hitting him where he lives. And you can see that he lives not that far from here. His home is just miles away."

Sparrow brightened. "This is most advantageous. Preordained perhaps. I would need to see exactly where he lives before I decide how to deal with him."

"Do you wish to visit his business as well?"

"Perhaps. But it may not be a good idea to reveal my hand at this point. I admit I am intrigued to come face to face with this McFadden, but if he has access to weapons I would be risking too much if he discovered my purpose."

"But he does not know you," she said.

"This is true. What would you suggest?"

"Perhaps you should consider looking at his home first."

"Yes. Let us start there." He picked up his porcelain cup and stared at Tala. "Will you accompany me?"

She hesitated. He reached out, lightly touching her arm. "It would mean much to me if you came."

Tala said, "Do you insist that I come with you?"

"I will not insist. But I think it would be better for my purpose if you were with me. Alone, I stand out. With you I become invisible."

"Very well. I honor my word."

"Tomorrow, then?"

"Yes, tomorrow we will find your man. I go with you on one condition."

"Name it."

"We take no weapons."

"Because?"

"If we were stopped for any reason, any reason at all, we would not raise suspicion. Just two people who appear to be...perhaps friends."

"Or lovers," teased Sparrow.

She blushed. "Perhaps. Do you agree about no weapons?"

"We do it your way. I am glad we will work together."

"I have a question," she said, brushing a lock of hair from her forehead.

He put down the teacup and waited.

"Do you not consider that you have been ill-served in this situation? What has this McFadden done that your patron sends you here with so little knowledge of the man you seek? Do you not find that strange?"

Sparrow shrugged. "Not at all. I am often given just a name and little else. I know that McFadden lives in this city, nothing more. I was told that I could ask for help once I got here. You have done exactly that. I now know not only where this McFadden lives but also that he has a business."

"And you think this is enough information?"

"I am certain to learn more, Tala."

"Very well. We will make this visit tomorrow. I think I have a way to get you very close to McFadden with almost no risk. But remember, no weapons. There will be no killing. What you decide to do later is not my concern."

"Agreed. Thank you for helping me."

"You earned it."

Chapter 16

Detective McManus spotted Mathis talking to two uniformed officers in the parking lot. He waved to Mathis and kept walking. Mathis broke ranks to hurry after him. "Morning, Mike. Got a hit on our airport gangbanger tour guide."

McManus waited for Mathis to catch up. "Good. You got a name?"

"Yeah. Manny Ramos."

"How'd you ID him?"

"One of our gang guys picked him out. Said Ramos's older brother was a real badass. Ran with the Insane Diego Mob and got put away for a string of nasty mom and pop stickups. Did some time, got out, went right back to what he knew. Got whacked in a drive-by a year ago."

McManus said, "And the younger brother, this Manny?"

"Pale imitation of big brother. Petty stuff. Somewhere between a wannabe and a made man. Our guys think he might be a gofer for Biggie Pacheco."

"And who's Biggie running with these days?"

"He was a wheel man for *Bahala Na Barkada*. Not sure he still runs with them. Rumor has it he sets up safe houses for someone these days."

"Can you pin that down?"

"I asked the gang guys to look into it. It would make sense if he was there to pick up our mystery man. Maybe the guy needed a place to stay."

McManus stared at the floor, thinking out loud. "Possible. Let's pick up this Ramos and squeeze him a little."

"Already on it. I think we should stroke him when we bring him in for a chat. My gut tells me he's a bottom feeder who'd like to think he's a genuine gangster."

McManus smiled. "I like it. Give Ramos the royal treatment but scare him enough to get something, anything on our visitor."

"Will do. Just so you know, Honolulu didn't have anything for us on this Ramon Reyes guy. Probably means the ink wasn't even dry on his alias."

"Makes sense. It was worth a try."

"Lunch?"

Glancing at his watch, McManus said, "Why not? Make it one. If I get out of my meeting earlier, I'll stop by your office. Maybe you'll be sitting on Manny Ramos by then."

Mathis grinned. "Hey, I could invite him to join us."

"Sure," replied McManus, "but only if I get to play Bad Cop."

Chapter 17

With his eyes closed, Wolf, barefooted, glided across the tiled patio between the guesthouse and the pool. Behind him, the distant outline of San Diego sat beneath another perfect china blue sky. Pivoting gracefully, left arm held out in front of him, horizontal with the ground, he flexed his left knee as if leaning into the wind. Wolf repeated the move, reversing the angle. Moving in slow motion to music only he could hear, Wolf rotated, his left foot now at ninety degrees to his torso.

Reggie McFadden slipped out the kitchen's sliding glass door and tiptoed to the patio. She placed a tray with two glasses and a pitcher of chilled orange juice on the glass table and stood in the umbrella's shade, watching Wolf's morning Tai Chi routine.

"Your morning OJ, *Jiàoshī*."

Wolf paused, breaking his concentration mid-move. He smiled. "I'm impressed, Reggie. Where did you learn to say 'teacher' in Chinese?"

"Sam taught me. Said it would put a smile on your face."

"He's right." He relaxed his pose and wandered to the table. "*Xiè xie*. Thanks for the treat."

"You're welcome. Show me how to perform *Strum the Pei Pa*."

"Ah, someone's been doing their homework." Wolf took a long sip of juice, put the glass down, and laughed.

"Pay attention, Grasshopper." He led her through the moves, their paired hands moving in unison as if in slow motion. He repeated the steps twice, then slapped her outstretched hand in a high-five salute.

Reggie giggled. "Do you exercise like this every day?"

"When I get the chance. By the way, I'm heading back east in ten days."

Reggie sipped her juice. "Sam told me. We'll miss you. I know he loves having you here. So do I. It's fun when you stay with us."

"Never a dull moment, eh?" Wolf dropped into a chair and finished his drink.

"Would love to hang around longer, Reggie. But I have to earn my pay. What's Sam up to anyway?" he asked.

She mimicked typing. "Slaving away in his office. Bunch of emails needed attention."

"No rest for the wicked, eh?"

"He's already had breakfast. He's not going to the shop until after lunch.

What are your plans?"

Wolf glanced at his watch. "I want to get in five miles around your lake this morning before it gets too hot. Then a swim in your pool, a nap, some reading, maybe some range time."

"Seriously? That's your agenda?"

"Absolutely. I'm not going to have this kind of down time again for a while."

"Then you should think about moving out here."

"Nice of you to say so, Reggie."

"I'm serious."

"Better to visit every so often and keep the friendship alive than to move here permanently and end up on your doorstep every day."

"Old Confucius saying?"

"Nah, my Old Man. He used to say, 'Relatives and fish —three days at the max and they both begin to stink.'"

"You're different. Just keep an open mind about moving."

She got up from the table and took the tray to the kitchen. Wolf ran through a dozen exercises before quitting. He retreated to the pool guesthouse and changed into jogging gear. Running shoes in hand, he returned to find McFadden waiting for him.

"Reggie says you're gonna put in five miles today."

Wolf knelt to tie his shoes. "I need it. Been slacking off this past week."

"Gonna make the circuit around Lake Miramar?"

Wolf stood. "Thought it would be as good a spot as any."

"Five miles. Take my car to the park if you'd like."

"Kinda defeats the purpose, doesn't it?"

"S'pose so," said McFadden. "But you'll be running two miles uphill on the way back."

"No pain, no gain," said Wolf.

"Your choice. Let's plan on some range time later."

Wolf grinned. "Love to. I'll get in a swim first. What a life, huh?"

"Not bad. But when I'm done with my chores I'll be sitting here poolside while you're down there, pounding pavement."

"I take it that means you're not coming with me."

McFadden threw an arm around his friend and smiled. "Would love to, Wolfman, but I'm only halfway through my emails and paperwork. Have to dot those I's and cross those T's."

"I feel your pain, Sam."

"And I have no intention of feeling yours."

McFadden crossed the patio to the house. "Take your cellphone," he said over his shoulder.

"So I can call paramedics if I need 'em?"

Laughing, McFadden shook his head, waved, and disappeared inside.

Wolf went back to his quarters and pocketed the phone. *Be prepared*, *scout*, he thought.

Chapter 18

Wolf took to the sidewalk, a solitary pedestrian leisurely trotting the two miles downhill alongside busy Scripps Ranch Boulevard. Above him, townhomes hugged near-vertical rocky hillsides overlooking the streaming traffic. He paced himself on the steep, winding grade, the return trip in mind.

Sam was right, he thought, *the jog back will inflict some punishment.* Wolf wore a ragged baseball cap, T-shirt, and loose sweats. He gripped a small bottle of water in his left hand, the cellphone zipped in a black case on one hip. He kept on, past the Mira Mesa light, lengthening his stride toward the lake's public park. The run felt good, his muscles responding to the steady pace. The blur of oncoming cars on his right was constant, not threatening, the sun warm, not yet scorching, and the cloudless sky a perfect San Diego blue.

Taking my time. What more could you ask? No chief running alongside, screaming at you to keep up. No backbreaking pack with salt-soaked straps cutting into shoulders already raw from previous runs. No cramping muscles knotted in agony. No sucking air into burning lungs starved for oxygen.

His running shoes hit pavement, not the shifting, punishing sand of Coronado's Strand. Wolf smiled at the memory of his BUD/S training.

What's not to like?

He jogged left at Scripps Lake Drive, aiming for the public park on the south side of Lake Miramar. Wolf trotted past the reservoir's fenced-in water treatment plant, through the parking lot, and paused to take a breather at the foot of a towering eucalyptus where he sipped water in the shade.

Across the shimmering lake, a line of houses, McFadden's among them, crowned the ridgeline of parched brown hills bristling with tall brush. Wolf stepped back to allow a string of riders on mountain bikes lap a flock of slow-moving seniors. Following in their wake, runners, paired or solitary, pounded the path, their limbs sweaty, their faces grim, determined.

Wolf took out his cellphone and called McFadden. "Sam, it's me," he said. "I'm standing in the parking lot, my eyes on your house. Thought I'd let you know I'm about to start my run."

"Don't let me hold you up then. I'm with you in spirit."

Wolf laughed. "I'll call you when I'm at the bottom of your hill."

"Do that," said McFadden. "Reggie and I will come out on the patio and wave to you in solidarity."

"Roger that." Wolf ended the call and glanced at his watch. Two bronzed, long-legged blondes in white sprinted by, catching his eye. He took a last sip of water, then set off to clock five miles on the serpentine pavement circling the lake. The worn maintenance road, off-limits to most vehicular traffic, had first appealed to him when he had seen cyclists and runners orbiting the lake daily from McFadden's patio high in the hills. Now it was his turn.

Yeah, what's not to like?

Keeping to the right of the road's faded yellow centerline, Wolf broke into a steady stride. The route was not particularly taxing. The lake's level had dropped significantly, leaving weedy shallows behind in finger-shaped inlets along the northern shoreline. At intervals, portable toilets stood like blue sentinels. Thirsty eucalyptus and scrubby pines threw scant shade along the roadway and scattered rocks lined the edge of the pavement like bleached bones. Speed limit signs cautioned cyclists not to exceed fifteen miles per hour. Stunted dusty palms clustered near the lake's marshy pockets.

The blondes in white were far ahead. No chance of catching them. As the number of people thinned, Wolf lapped solitary walkers. He was overtaken in turn by cyclists, who then charged into the foothills on hard-packed spidery paths through the parched brush.

Tempted to explore the challenging off-road trails, Wolf nonetheless kept to the roadway until he reached a spot below the bluff where McFadden's house perched, barely visible in the tinder-dry undergrowth.

Wolf stopped, drank some water, and pulled out his phone. About to call McFadden, he paused, his attention distracted by two climbers halfway up the hill. He followed a crooked footpath to a bald rise of rock and scanned the brush above for a better look. The scrambling figures had reached a point just below the crest of the hill. Wolf eyed the pair as they skirted an empty home next door to McFadden's. The neighbor's house, Sam had told him, was in the midst of a month-long stalled renovation due to a dispute with the contractor. Wolf tapped the phone's screen, got McFadden on the second ring.

"Hey, Wolfman, what's up? You doing okay in this heat?"

"Doing fine, Sam. I like the heat. I'm right below your place."

"Great. You're making good time."

"Yeah. Say, you should know you've got visitors."

"Really? Explain."

Wolf tracked the pair. They were definitely headed for Sam's house. "I'm watching two people on the slope just below your backyard."

"You're positive?"

"Absolutely. Right now they look to be about fifty, sixty yards from your fence."

"Thanks, Wolfman. I'll look into it."

"Roger that. Want me to stand by?"

"Keep an eye on them for me. If they find a blind spot, let me know."

"Okay, you've got about five minutes before they're knocking on your kitchen door, Sam."

"I'll call you back."

Wolf moved to the shade of a stunted tree on the edge of a draw where he couldn't be seen. From his vantage point he could follow McFadden's trespassers.

Whoever you are, people, be prepared for a rude awakening.

Chapter 19

McFadden grabbed a Beretta from his office gun safe, loaded it, and slipped it in his waistband underneath a loose aloha shirt. He called upstairs, alerting Reggie, and went into the kitchen to get two small bottles of water from the fridge. McFadden went outside to the patio and scanned the drop-off just beyond the edge of his fenced backyard. Nothing. No sign of anyone heading his way. He dropped the bottles near the gate leading to the hillside, uncoiled a garden hose, and moved to the metal fence marking his property. McFadden began spraying a thick carpet of ice plant he had seeded the year before to hold the hillside.

In minutes, he spotted movement to his left, on the slope below. Wolf had been right. Two people. A man and woman. The pair, unaware McFadden had seen them, parted the brush and crabbed their way across the last ten yards of exposed rocky ground, the stones loose beneath their feet.

"You folks lost?"

McFadden, one hand sweeping the nozzle across the vegetation, the other at his hip, close to the Beretta, stared at his unwelcome guests. An awkward silence followed.

Surprised by McFadden, the woman, face partially hidden by a wide straw hat and sunglasses, finally spoke. "Oh, hello. We saw the house next door and wanted a closer look." She waved at the scaffolding hugging the neighbor's house.

Eyeing the woman's companion, a slight brown man, also wearing sunglasses and dark clothing but no hat, McFadden said, "Not for sale. This is all private property."

"We were not aware of that," she said. "My apologies."

McFadden shut off the nozzle, dropped the hose, and picked up the water bottles. "You should know that this entire ridge is private property," he said, sweeping his arm across the ridge. "Technically you're trespassing."

"We meant no harm," she said.

He tossed one water bottle to her. "Here, you must be thirsty." She caught the bottle and underhanded it to the man behind her.

McFadden threw her the second bottle. "You know, the sun."

"Yes, of course," she said. "The sun. How thoughtful of you."

"You're welcome." He locked eyes with her. "Take the water with you on your way back down."

She uncapped the bottle and made a show of swallowing. The silent man did the same. "Yes, we'll be going now," she said.

"I'm sure you will," said McFadden. "Be careful. There are loose rocks...and rattlesnakes as well."

"Rattlesnakes?" She looked around her feet.

"Yeah. We have an understanding, the snakes and I." His eyes bored into hers. "They don't come in the yard. They know better."

"Thank you for the warning, sir."

"No problem. You two take care now...on your way back."

She raised the bottle to her lips, drank, then capped it. "We'll go now."

McFadden didn't move. He stood at his gate, staring at the couple as they worked their way back the way they had come. When the pair reached the trail taken to gain the crest of the hill, the woman turned and waved. McFadden did not return the gesture. Instead, he called Wolf.

"Wolfman. They're headed back your way. Can you see them?"

"Got 'em."

"Okay. Take a good look when they pass."

"Can do. I'll get back on the road and wait for them."

McFadden leaned on the railing, his eyes on the ant-like figures bobbing in the dry brush. "Could have been an innocent mistake. Maybe curiosity on their part."

"Kinda odd when you think about it, Sam."

"Yeah, maybe. One more thing."

"I'm listening."

"If you want to cut short your run, you can climb this way."

"How do I know you won't send me back down the hill once I get up there?"

McFadden laughed. "You don't."

Wolf said, "Got a better idea. How about I follow your mountaineers once they get down here? I can track them to their car. Get a license number. Maybe get some shots of them with my cellphone if I can get close enough."

"Great idea. But don't let them know you've made them."

"Trust me. I can play the game."

Chapter 20

Wolf, back from tailing McFadden's trespassers, peeled off the sweat-soaked T-shirt and mopped his torso and neck. "Filipinos."

McFadden, seated at a poolside table shaded by an umbrella, said, "You're sure?"

"Dawg, we both know Filipinos when we see them." Grateful for the shade, Wolf dropped into a chair across from McFadden.

"Actually, the whole parking lot was full of them. I was in the minority."

McFadden uncapped a fresh San Miguel from the cooler at his feet. "Yeah, obviously up from Mira Mesa—we call it Manila Mesa. The cops call it Mecca Town for some reason." He took a pull on his beer. "The park and road around the reservoir are popular spots with the locals."

"That pair in your backyard looked harmless enough. What's your take?"

McFadden shook his head. "Reggie thinks they were casing the joint."

"Odd way to do it. Easier to just cruise your street. You're not gated."

"True. Maybe they already have."

"A possibility," said Wolf. "Man, I need to cool off." He got up and walked to the pool. Facing McFadden, he backed down the steps, his hand on the rail. "If I hadn't been on foot I could have trailed them after they drove away." Wolf pushed off the steps and drifted toward the deep end, his head above water.

McFadden raised his bottle. "Hey, getting that cellphone picture of their license plate was good enough. I just sent it to a friend in the cop shop."

"Outstanding. That oughta tell us something."

Wolf submerged and began doing underwater laps. At the end of the fourth one he surfaced, refreshed, the Filipino couple momentarily forgotten. "I'm gonna miss this, Sam."

"Reggie says she tried to talk you into staying."

"Yeah, but just a few more days and I'm back at it. Duty calls."

"After dinner we've got an appointment with some targets."

"Good. Reggie coming along?"

"Nah. For someone who's a good shot, she's not that excited about range time. Just you and me."

Wolf floated on his back. "Care to wager a few bucks?"

"Don't want to take your money, Wolfman."

"How about whoever has the best head grouping wins?"

"Fine. Nine shots max. May the best man win."

Reggie came to the patio door and called. "Sam, someone from the police department on the phone for you."

McFadden got up from his chair. "Might be info on that license plate you spotted."

Treading water, Wolf said, "See if you can get the number for the woman. She's a keeper."

"At ease, sailor."

Wolf laughed. "I'm just saying..."

McFadden watched Wolf go under and went inside to take the call.

In ten minutes he returned with his cellphone, waving for Wolf's attention. Climbing from the pool, Wolf toweled off and joined McFadden at the table.

"We got a hit. Expired plates belonging to a pickup in Imperial Beach."

Wolf helped himself to a beer. "Wasn't a pickup, Sam."

McFadden stroked his chin. "Yeah, so you said. Something funny, huh?"

"I know my cars," said Wolf. "It was definitely a white Toyota Highlander.

Little bit of rust on both rear wheel wells."

"I believe you. Stolen plates. Not good. I'm not liking this."

"You get a lot of break-in calls up here on Mount Olympus?"

"Maybe one in the three years we've been here."

Wolf waved his bottle in the house's direction. "But like I said, you're not a gated community."

"True. It's never really been a problem except that one time."

"The cops catch the burglar?"

"Nope."

"I'm thinking it looks like easy pickings up here."

"Between Reggie and me, anybody who sets foot in our house is gonna be in a world of hurt."

"No one's saying these idiots are bright bulbs, Sam."

McFadden got up to pace. "You know, that pair may have been taking a close look at our neighbor's place. It's just sitting there for the taking."

Wolf wiped his mouth with the back of his hand. He shook his head. "Hate to say it, Sam, but those two were definitely heading for your house. No two ways about it." He chopped the air with his hand. "They made a beeline up the hill, didn't even stop to look next door."

"What do we have, then? A car, a phony license plate, and two burglar wannabes. Not much to go on. Plus, those pictures you took were a bit grainy and would fit most of Mira Mesa."

"Shame on me for not introducing myself. Guess you'll just have to be on your toes. You should let your neighborhood know about this."

"Good idea. Reggie knows everyone. I'll get her to call."

Wolf frowned. "Damn. I should have taken some better shots of the people in that car. I got to the lot before them and killed time until they showed. Didn't want them to know I made them. What was I thinking?"

"Don't beat yourself up about it. At least we have one advantage."

"And that would be?"

"I know they're out there...and I'll be waiting."

Chapter 21

Kearny Business Plaza

The polite young man in the blue golf shirt eyed the couple approaching his glass-topped counter. On the wall behind him hung mounted assault rifles, targets, shotguns, and posters of SEALs and Green Berets posing with weapons. He finished tying a small red sales tag to a Glock's trigger guard.

"Be with you in a moment, folks."

Sparrow nodded. He leaned to study the pistols, his fingers caressing the long glass display case as the clerk placed the Glock among the Berettas, Colts, shiny semi-automatics, and revolvers. Sparrow studied the collection of pistols behind the glass. The clerk locked the case and spread his hands on the countertop.

"Good afternoon. How can I help you?"

A moment of awkward silence. Tala smiled at the clerk's welcome. Sparrow, solemn, took his eyes from the case, straightened, and said, "We're interested in shooting. Would that be possible?"

"Of course. Have either of you visited our ranges before?"

"No."

The clerk launched into the range protocol. "Okay. As first-time shooters, I'll need to see your driver's licenses. We make copies for our records. That way you'll be able to skip this step next time you come in to use the range."

"I see." Sparrow fished a wallet from his back pocket and handed over his license. He motioned to Tala at his elbow. "The lady won't be shooting."

"Okay."

"But may she watch me on the range?"

"Yes. There is a yellow line on the floor behind the lanes for those not actively shooting. It's standard procedure."

"That will be fine."

"Good. We require everyone to watch our safety video. It's a five-minute piece. For safety's sake, you understand."

"Oh, of course."

He ushered the two to chairs in a windowless room with a flat-screen TV.

After hitting a button to begin the video, the counter clerk left to run a copy of Sparrow's license and answer the phone. When the safety film ended, Sparrow and Tala returned to the counter. Sparrow was given back his license and handed a clipboard with a single sheet of paperwork to fill out.

"Standard profile questions," said the clerk. "Address, phone number, email address, and stuff. Just fill in the appropriate boxes. This information remains with us and will not be shared beyond this office."

As Sparrow scribbled, the clerk said, "What would you like to shoot today?"

"What handguns would you recommend?" asked Sparrow.

"For a first time shooter, maybe something a bit lighter, a Beretta."

"How many rounds do you suggest?"

"Well, for starters, I'd say three magazines. That's thirty-six rounds. Ian, our range safety officer, will show you how to load. He'll also ready the targets. Any questions, ask Ian."

"Thank you," said Sparrow. "You're very thorough."

"We try to be. Safety is our primary concern."

Tala said, "That's reassuring."

The counter clerk handed both padded earmuffs. He smiled at Tala. "Ma'am, you should use these when you're watching him. The sound will be quite loud for someone not used to gunfire."

A dazzling smile. Tala said, "Thank you. I appreciate the warning."

Sparrow and Tala were introduced to Ian and followed him into the handgun range. In a patient monotone, the blue-shirted range officer showed Sparrow how to load a magazine, how to chamber the first round, and work the safety. Again and again, he emphasized the possible dangers of live firing. That done, he hung a target for Sparrow and sent it seven yards downrange. He stood behind Sparrow and watched him fire three rounds. Satisfied with Sparrow's ability to handle the weapon, he excused himself to monitor shooters in adjacent lanes.

Sparrow went through three magazines and put down the Beretta. Signaling Ian, he left the Beretta aimed downrange and thanked him for introducing him to the range.

"Most enjoyable," he said. "I look forward to my next outing."

"Glad you enjoyed your experience, sir." With a wink at Tala, Ian said, "Perhaps you'll give it a try next time, ma'am."

A blushing Tala smiled. "Oh, no. I don't think so. Too loud for me."

Sparrow pointed at the Beretta. "Do we return the pistol to the counter?"

"Not a problem. I'll take care of the firearm, sir. Visit us again."

"Certainly." The pair surrendered their earmuffs, paid in cash, and left.

Chapter 22

Tom Wolf entered the gun range's lobby, passing the exiting couple, giving them the briefest of glances. He sauntered to the counter to sign in when he had second thoughts about the two. Pen paused above the log sheet, he asked, "Tony, who were those folks who just left?"

The clerk looked up from his keyboard. "The Hispanic couple?"

"I figured them for Filipino. But, yeah, those people."

Tony turned, asking Ian, who had just left the range carrying a plastic bin with the Beretta and empty magazines. "Hey, who was that couple you had in the range just now?"

"Dunno. A new shooter. Check the sign-in sheet."

Scanning the clipboard, Wolf beat him to it. "Signature is Ramon Reyes."

"Yeah, that's him," said Tony. "The girl with him didn't shoot, just the guy."

Wolf was torn. "Sam in the office?"

"As far as I know. Why?"

Wolf hurried to the lobby, saying over his shoulder, "Call Sam. Tell him his visitors just showed up. He'll understand." At the door to the parking lot he yelled, "Ian, don't touch that pistol until I get back!"

Bursting through the door, Wolf searched the parked cars. Racing the length of the lot without spotting the couple, he jogged to the street, looking both ways at passing traffic. *Too late*, he thought. *Damn, I know that was them.*

When Wolf trudged through the door McFadden was talking with Ian and Tony. The three faced an agitated Wolf.

"Visitors?" said McFadden. "What the hell are you talking about? You spooked my guys."

Waving his arm in the direction of the lot, Wolf said, "Those two who made the house call the other day. It's them. The people climbing the hill."

"You're sure?"

"I remember the woman for sure," said Wolf. "I think the guy with her was the same one in your backyard that day."

McFadden's brow darkened. He turned the sign-in sheet clipboard to scan the names. "Ramon Reyes. California license. Should be easy to check the name and address."

Wolf said, "Wanna bet it's a phony name?"

"I hear you."

"Geez, if I had known," reddened the clerk. "They looked okay."

"At ease, Tony," said McFadden. "No way you would have known."

Wolf glanced at Ian. "Did you touch the pistol?"

Holding up both hands, the range officer said, "Negative."

"Then we've got the sonofabitch, Sam. Get your friends in the cop shop to dust for prints."

"On the basis of what? My suspicion that this guy might be a burglar?"

"What? You don't think this is serious?"

"Didn't say that. I only meant that we have nothing to go on."

Wolf's eyebrows danced. "Hey, isn't this the guy and his lady who were driving a car with stolen plates the day they did the uninvited recon on your home? Isn't that what your cop buddies told you?"

McFadden conceded the point. "Sorry, I blanked on that. You're right. We can ask." He pointed at his range chief. "Ian, take that Beretta out of circulation until I can find out if the cops are willing to check for prints."

"Will do, Sam." Ian set aside the plastic bin as if it were toxic.

McFadden barked out another order. "And guys, if this pair shows again, call me immediately. Stall em if you have to. Don't let them anywhere near a handgun or ammo."

Wolf added, "And tell the new shift the same thing. Its obvious these two are up to no good. They've already scoped out Sam's house."

"That true, Sam?" said Ian.

"It is," said McFadden. "I sent them back down the hill myself."

"They were two minutes from showing up at his back door," fumed Wolf. "As for today—"

Interrupting, McFadden said, "For them to show up here at the business adds to the seriousness of what Wolfman's saying. Be alert, guys."

Tony was wary, asking, "But business goes on as usual, right?"

"Absolutely. No changes. Take care of our legit clients."

"What about security cameras?" said Wolf.

"Good idea. Ian, check the feeds from the lobby, parking lot, and range cameras. These two have to show up. We can use those to familiarize the staff, and the cops might want to see them."

Wolf repeatedly slammed his fist in his hand. "Why didn't I see this sooner? I could have confronted them. Coulda done something."

"It happens," snapped McFadden. "Leave it."

"Won't happen again, Sam. You've got my word on that."

"Good enough for me, Wolfman."

Chapter 23

Fueled by his second cup of coffee, a personal defeat, McManus pecked at his keyboard. His cellphone buzzed. Mathis calling. He tapped the speaker button. "Don't you ever sleep?" he said.

Mathis laughed. "Sleep's overrated."

"So you say. Okay, what's the reason for your obvious cheerfulness?"

"Guess who I'm sitting with, Mike?"

"You know I hate guessing games," groused McManus. "Give it up."

"Remember that low-life we're looking for, the guy from the airport?"

"Yeah, Manny Nirano, or something like that."

"Ramos," said Mathis.

"I stand corrected. Manny Ramos. Tell me you're sitting across from him and you've read him his rights."

"Sorry to disappoint you, Mike. But it's still good news. I'm having lunch with Karen Little."

McManus said, "The mouthy blonde who used to work gangs?"

"That's her. She's working juvenile probation these days."

"Good for her, but why should I be interested?"

Mathis chuckled. "Because she ran into some of her friends from the street gang unit last night. She heard about us asking them to be on the lookout for Manny Ramos. Karen knows this guy. Confirms he's a gofer for Biggie Pacheco, a runner. Says he does everything except pick up Biggie's socks from the floor."

"She know where we can find this guy?"

"Affirmative. When he's not shadowing Biggie, Ramos's side job is ripping off sucker bettors in Mecca Town. She said he's got a little gambling thing going for himself just off Mira Mesa Boulevard. Runs his game in one of those cheap pre-paid cellphone storefronts. I got the address."

Intrigued, McManus abandoned the keyboard. "How good's her intel?"

"Karen knows her stuff. Says Ramos gives her tips on some of her kids in the system from time to time."

McManus snorted. "A real upstanding citizen, huh?"

"She cut Ramos some slack a couple years ago and he seems to feel he owes her. Apparently, he doesn't want kids to end up like he did."

"You're breaking my heart, Bob. Say the word and I can have a couple units meet you at the phone shop. They can bring in Ramos for a chat."

"Karen says he's in over his head with the gang thing. His brother was the real deal, a bad ass, but this guy's a pussycat."

"Your call, Bob. Would she be willing to help us with this guy?"

Mathis paused, his voice vague in the background. He came back on. "She'd be willing to talk to him if we run him downtown, but she doesn't want to burn that bridge if she doesn't have to."

"I understand," McManus said. "But what if we can steer him into asking for her? You know, play the bad cop card and then ask if he'd rather talk to someone else."

"How about this," said Mathis. "Maybe she passes me in the hallway when I'm bringing him in. She could act surprised, stop me, and ask why he's there. She'd be a friendly face. He's dumb enough to go for it."

Warming to the idea, McManus said, "Worth a try. Ask her." He drained the remaining coffee and tossed the cup while waiting for Mathis to pitch the setup to Karen Little.

"Okay, we're good," said Mathis. "She thinks it might work. I'm gonna recon the phone shop and see if Ramos's there. If he is, I'll call you ASAP and you can have a patrol bag him. Karen says she's got some stops downtown anyway so this could work if we time it right."

McManus liked the idea. "Good. I'll be waiting for your call. We'll coordinate with Karen when our little friend is en route. You savvy?"

"I can't wait," said Mathis. "I predict this guy will fold."

"Willing to bet lunch?"

"Why not?" said Mathis. "You're on. Hey, if this works, you owe Karen and me both. You game?"

"Sure. We'll see just how good you are."

"I'm so devious it scares me sometimes."

"It should."

Chapter 24

Wolf took out his frustration on targets while McFadden made some calls. They both ended up better for their efforts. Wolf focused his anger on paper, keeping his groups centered and tight, alternating between a Beretta and a Glock. McFadden, meanwhile, connected with Detective Mike McManus, an old friend in the police department's intelligence division.

"Sam, long time, no hear," said McManus. "Some of the SWAT boys told me they had a good time at your indoor paintball range. I'd love to get my kid out there one of these days."

"Book a time as my guest, Mike. Your kid would probably give you a run for your money. Might even embarrass you."

McManus chuckled. "Tell me about it. What's going on with you?"

"Got a mystery on my hands."

"Tell the nice officer what's bothering you."

"This may be nothing or it could be the start of something serious."

"Which is it?"

McFadden paused, groping for the right words. "Not sure. You tell me. The strangest thing happened a few days ago. Remember my friend Tom Wolf?"

"Your houseguest, the former SEAL? How could I forget him? He left me with some unanswered questions in my lap about that Russian mob thing you were involved in two years ago."

McFadden got up from his desk and paced. "He was innocent, as pure as the driven snow, Mike."

"So you say. He always seems to be in the thick of it...whatever 'it' was. So, what's his role in this latest thing?"

"That's the odd thing. He's not part of my problem. Actually, he's been helpful."

"Okay, lay it out for me. What are we talking about here?"

"Wolf's staying with Reggie and me. He was here for the open house at the new range. One day last week he was jogging around Lake Miramar."

"Nice real estate, if I remember. Part of the Old Scripps Ranch, right?"

"That's it. On the home stretch that day Wolf called me to say there were two people climbing the hill below my house."

"I know the geography. Not illegal to my knowledge."

"True. But the top of the ridge is all private property. No public access. Wolf claimed these folks were definitely headed for my house."

"And?"

"I went out in the backyard and confronted them. Warned them they were trespassing."

"What happened?"

"They apologized. Said they didn't realize it, and climbed back down."

"End of story?"

"Not quite. Wolf watched them come down and followed them to the park's lot. He got some shots of their car and license plate. Took some pictures of them before they left."

"I'm gonna guess there's more to this tale."

"Right. I called your shop and asked a friend to check on the plates."

"Stolen, right?"

"Exactly. How did you know?"

"I'm not shocked. Your voice gave it away. So, you think these two were targeting your house? Maybe a couple professionals looking for a soft target? Of course, knowing you, they wouldn't find one."

"Roger that."

"Always have to be careful with that, Sam. I know a man's home is his castle but you know how things are these days. Hey, not that I agree."

"I'm aware of that. I'm always careful."

"It's a little sketchy, Sam. What do you want me to do?"

"What about Wolf's pictures of the license and the car?"

"Email me. I can have a couple units keep an eye open for the car."

Phone to his ear, McFadden perched on the corner of his desk. "But there's one more thing."

"Something to hang a hat on?"

"An odd thing. Yesterday, this same couple shows up at my range and does some shooting."

A low whistle from McManus's end of the phone. "Whoa, that's either very stupid or very ballsy."

"Maybe both. Only the guy did the shooting."

"So we're talking about a woman as the other half now?"

"Yeah. Forgot to mention that. It gets better. They finished shooting and left. Wolf passed them on his way in. By the time the light bulb went on for him, the couple had vanished."

"He's positive these two were your climbers?"

McFadden sank on a leather couch against one wall of his office. "One hundred percent sure."

McManus sighed. "So much for his observation skills, Sam."

"Cut him some slack. These people were completely out of context."

"Okay, but still..."

McFadden sighed. "Yeah, I know, he's banging his head against the wall for letting them slip away."

McManus said, "I'm making some notes as we speak." He asked, "Your shooters have to sign in, don't they? Show a license, right?"

"SOP. This shooter followed our protocol."

"You make copies when they do that?"

"Only for first timers. After that, it's a sign-in policy."

"But they still show a license, correct?"

"Yes, each time."

"You have a name and a picture then."

"I do."

"Okay. Let's hope it's legit, though I have a funny feeling. Give me the details, then scan it, and attach it in an email. I'll get the ball rolling."

McFadden recited the name, address, and license number.

"Wait a minute, Sam. Let me see if I got this name right. Did you say, Ramon Reyes?"

"That's correct. You know that name?"

"Yeah, I think so. Let me be politically incorrect for a moment, okay? Was this guy Filipino by chance?"

"Yeah, both of them. Guess I forgot to mention that. Wolf confirmed it when he trailed them in the parking lot. What's going on, Mike?"

"Sam, for now I'll just say we have a very odd coincidence here. A lucky break. Maybe the stars are lined up or something, if you believe that crap. I'm going to talk to some people here and get right back to you. You gonna be around?"

"Not planning on going anywhere. Should I be worried?"

"Hmm, not sure yet. But I'd say you might want to watch your back until I have something more definite for you, okay?"

"I'll do that. Keep me posted."

"Will do. Oh, and Sam—"

"I'm listening."

"Keep Wolf close to you."

McFadden's brow furrowed. "That serious, huh?"

"I'm just saying..."

McManus rang off, called Mathis, got his voicemail, and left a hurried message. "Bob, get back to me ASAP. We have a big problem."

For good measure, he sent a text, something he was normally loath to do.

Chapter 25

Sparrow was flying high, Tala furious. The risk they had taken by visiting McFadden's range ignited a slow burn building inside her. Retreating to a rattan chair in the lanai's corner, she sulked. Finally gathering her nerve, she said, "It was foolish to tempt fate before its time. When I agreed to help you I did not think you would act so recklessly."

Her reproof fell on deaf ears. Sparrow still glowed with the memory of violating his prey's home and business. "Think of it, Tala. We have faced the man I have come to kill. Faced him in his own home."

She scoffed. "It was his backyard, not exactly his home. And we were at his mercy. You seem to forget that he showed no fear."

"Of course not," he snapped. "McFadden was armed and at your insistence we were not. Perhaps you missed that detail."

"I saw his pistol. Now do you understand why I said I would only accompany you if we went unarmed? What chance would we have stood had he decided to kill us both?"

"I will admit I first thought your idea sound. But when he appeared before us we could have taken him had we been armed. This matter would have been done with."

"In daylight? I think that would have been a bad idea."

"Daylight is no problem for me," he said.

Shaking her head, Tala refused to celebrate what she considered a close call. "It was bad enough to risk visiting his home. I still cannot believe I let you talk me into going to his shooting range."

He brushed away her concern. "You had a choice, dear Tala. Admit that you enjoyed the game."

"I admit nothing except that you are foolish to continue to move about in daylight as if you had nothing to fear. Do you not care that you had to show your license? You know nothing of how our police operate. Do you admit it?"

Sparrow ran a hand through his oiled hair and dropped into the chair opposite, the faintest of smiles on his lips. "Police are the same regardless of where they serve."

She showed her sarcastic side. "Oh, so now the worldly citizen speaks as though he knows everything. You have no idea how the San Diego Police operate. You think they don't know about our activities? Biggie Pacheco has been arrested numerous times for things he has done. They know who he is. They may even know of us soon enough."

"And you, my dear Tala. How often have the police arrested you?"

She bristled. "Not once have I been suspected of being anything other than a proper citizen. It is my armor. Up until you arrived I did not risk being in a position where police might want to talk to me."

He gestured to the house and walled yard. "You think you are invisible because you stay out of sight here in your 'safe house' serving only when called upon? Don't fool yourself, Tala. When the time comes, you will have to make a choice: retreat like a coward or take the fight to the enemy and vanquish them."

"You make such boastful words, *pinoy*. You are only a guest here on a mission. Once you accomplish your goal you will leave. We are the ones who stay behind, who take the risk by having you under our roof."

"You are obligated," he said in a flat voice.

"I am not obligated to accompany you on your suicide mission."

Sparrow got up to pace. "I can't believe this is the same woman who exhibited such skill with *yantoks*. You were fearless in attack. You asked for no quarter and gave none. You acquitted yourself well. Why has your courage suddenly left you? Where is the Tala I faced in this garden? Where is the woman who comes to me at night? Has she been replaced by a child?"

"I only warn you of the risks you seem determined to ignore."

"Risks? You talk to me of risks? Every day of my life has been a risk, Tala. This is the last risk I take—the killing of this Sam McFadden."

"And then what? You leave us to return to Manila to a life of ease?"

He pointed a finger at her. "Ah, that is my secret, Tala. I am not returning to Manila. There are reasons I cannot go back. Like Americans say, I have burned my bridge behind me. For me, there is no going back."

Puzzled, she said, "Then maybe you should abandon your mission. If you insist on going through with it you may not succeed. Have you considered that?"

Hands clasped behind his back, Sparrow closed his eyes and tilted his head to the sun. "I will succeed. I have never failed. I will not fail now. And when I am finished with McFadden I will vanish like I always have."

"Just like that, eh?"

He turned to her. "I am *multo*, dear Tala. You know this word?"

"A spirit."

Sparrow smiled. "Yes, but a spirit that kills. McFadden will never see me coming. I will strike and be gone before he even knows he is dying."

"And then?"

"And then...we will celebrate, dear Tala. I will be a rich man."

"When are you planning to do this?"

"Soon. We must return to McFadden's house."

"That's crazy. He knows what we look like."

"It does not matter. It has to be at his house and not his gun range. There are too many people to take him there. Too many guns against my one. No, his home is the best place. We will be waiting for him when he returns at the end of day."

"There may be others at his home, perhaps a wife or family."

He smiled. "Good. We can use them to draw him in."

Chapter 26

Detective Bob Mathis kept his left hand on the wheel, a cellphone in his right. He read the text from McManus but ignored it for the time being, focusing instead on the business at hand. He got out of the car and headed inside the cellphone store where two uniformed officers had collared Manny Ramos. The gang member, patted down but defiant, had assumed the position against a wall in the betting shop masquerading as a phone shop.

A cocky Ramos challenged the cops. "Why am I being arrested?"

Mathis spilled a paper bag's contents on the store's glass counter. Betting slips, IOUs and crumpled, soiled cash. "You have a license for this?" A sullen Ramos kept silent. "I didn't think so," said Mathis. "It's a no-brainer, Manny. Secondly, you're a known gang member conducting illegal business."

"Hey, I found that bag under the counter. Belongs to somebody else."

The two officers holding Ramos did their best to keep their faces neutral. Mathis scooped the paper and cash back in the paper bag and shook it in Ramos's face. "Evidence, Manny. You're looking at five years minimum."

Despite first paling at the news, Ramos recovered and struck an insolent pose, his jaw thrust out.

"We're going for a ride," said Mathis. "Gonna have a chat downtown."

"I didn't do nothing."

"You been watching too many cop shows, Manny."

Mathis turned solemn. "Taking people's hard-earned cash for this phony racket? I've seen judges put people away for much less. You're going down, mister." He sent a cuffed, protesting Ramos away with a nod to the patrolmen. Once his pathetic prey was in the squad car's back seat, Mathis called over the officers.

"Take the long way downtown. I need at least thirty minutes to get my chess pieces in place. Call me when you're inbound. McManus and I will intercept you in the sally port and take it from there."

"You got it."

"Thanks for the help," said Mathis. "Remember, give me a heads-up."

"Not a problem."

A worried-looking Manny Ramos sank in the squad car's back seat, his bravado crumbling by the minute. By the time he was delivered downtown, Mathis knew he and McManus would be primed and waiting in ambush.

Mathis got in his car and left before the cops.

Downtown, Mathis found McManus waiting for him. "You called for backup. Did the squad find him?"

Mathis waved off McManus to take a call. Nodding, he said, "Ten minutes away."

"Ramos?"

"Yep. Got him at that phone shop. I told the squad to take their time getting here. We need to be ready. You good?"

"Better than good, Bob, we got a break. I think I know what our mystery man is up to. Did you get my text?"

"I did. Sorry I couldn't get back to you right away. You know, Ramos. You look like a kid at Christmas, Mike. So talk."

"Sam McFadden."

"What about him?"

McManus jabbed a finger in his partner's chest. "This guy's after Sam McFadden. A month's pay says he's here to whack McFadden."

"Wait a minute," said Mathis. "Where's that coming from?"

"Talked to Sam an hour ago. Couple days ago he confronted two Filipinos, a man and a woman, in his backyard above Miramar Lake. They were about to make themselves at home when he stopped them. Sent 'em back down the hill."

"Okay, how does that translate into a sure thing?"

"Because he got a license number and cellphone pictures of these people. Our shop ran the plates. Stolen from another vehicle."

Mathis's expression didn't change. "I'll play devil's advocate. Tie it together for me."

"Same two showed up at his range two days later and did some shooting."

"And?"

"After their session, they vanished. Sounds to me like they were doing a dry run. McFadden's friend, Tom Wolf, ID'd the pair as the same two who paid a visit to Sam's house."

"Okay. It's possible. Kinda circumstantial, though."

"Sure, at this point. But don't you see? It fits. McFadden sent me files of the paperwork from the range that the Filipino guy filled out in order to shoot. License, signature, the whole nine yards. The guy's name was Ramon Reyes."

Mathis beamed. "Okay, now you've got my attention."

McManus sighed. "Geez, finally. Did you hear anything I said before that?"

"Yeah. I heard you. Everything you said sounds plausible."

McManus leaned against the wall. "Gotta think...next step."

"Then our next step," said Mathis, "is to squeeze Manny Ramos about the whereabouts of this guy."

McManus nodded. "We have got to nail down the phantom's location."

"We'll make it work," said Mathis, glancing out a window. "Put on your best face. Here come our guys. I'll go meet them."

Chapter 27

After small talk with the incoming officers, Mathis took the handoff from the patrolmen and marched a handcuffed Ramos through the watch commander's office to an elevator. On the fourth floor, a discreet McManus hung back, watching the choreographed interception by Karen Little in the hallway. As predicted, the gangster wannabe spotted her and called out.

After a few minutes of Mathis solemnly explaining the reason for Ramos's being there, she persuaded him to let her speak with his prisoner in one of the homicide unit's interrogation rooms. Shrugging, Mathis played his part well, reluctantly releasing Ramos to Karen Little.

It took forty minutes for Ramos to fold. A rap on the locked door brought Mathis, who let her out. The two walked down the hallway out of earshot. McManus waited at a table near a bank of vending machines. He offered to buy Little a cup of coffee.

"No thanks," she said, "I'm trying to quit. It's going on two weeks."

"Tell me your secret," said McManus.

Mathis rolled his eyes. "We're on the clock, Mike."

"Okay," said McManus, clearing his throat. "Let's hear what your little gangbanger friend had to say, Karen."

"I told him I'd talk to you. Try to get him released without charge."

McManus shook his head. "How good is the info he gave you? I don't want to let him walk without something to go on."

"It's good, Mike," she said. "I believe him. It's the product of a fertile mind but I think most of it is true."

"I'm listening," he said. "Sell me."

"Manny's just a gofer for Biggie," she said. "And right now, Biggie's latest thing is running a couple of safe houses in Mecca Town for the gangs."

"Mira Mesa's a haystack. Does he know addresses?" said McManus.

"He only knows the one where he stays. These places have apparently been declared neutral ground by the gangs. Sort of like the old cities of refuge."

McManus nodded to Mathis. "We've heard the rumors. Let's double-check this with the gang guys. It's a new twist. Can't see gangbangers doing this."

While Karen Little continued, Mathis tapped out a text to a friend in the street gang unit to verify her theory about the safe house agreement.

"Who knows how long this arrangement will last," she said. "But for now, this is their attempt to fly under our radar. Cooler heads apparently want to solve their own problems, mete out their justice without sparking wars."

McManus voiced more skepticism. "And a guy like Ramos knows all this? C'mon, he's a bottom feeder, Karen. Is he making this up?"

"No, he's sincere, Mike. Oh, he does stupid human tricks but he's not dumb. He's overheard enough about the arrangement to piece it together."

"That's interesting, Karen," McManus said, "but the real reason we're curious about your guy is because last week he showed up at the airport to welcome a mystery guest. We want to know who the newcomer is. We want to know where he went and what Ramos's connection is."

Mathis added, "Here's our problem: We have a name, Ramon Reyes. Only, we know it's an alias."

"Turns out he's driving a car with stolen plates," said McManus, "and was seen casing a home near Lake Miramar with an accomplice, a woman. Both of them later showed up at a gun range run by this same homeowner. The woman is an unknown but we have photos of both from security cameras. We spread the pictures around. No hits yet. We're hoping Ramos might be the key."

She said, "Maybe this pair is targeting the range to score some guns."

"Could be," said McManus, leaning forward, elbows on the table. "Your guy say anything about a mystery man?"

"He did mention someone. I thought he was trying to impress me. He thinks a guy who flew in from Hawaii is definitely well connected, maybe a hit man."

"Great. Just what we need in town. What does he base that on?"

"Like I said, he hears a lot more than the people around him realize. He said this guy calls himself Sparrow."

"Is this supposed hit man in our city to whack someone or just passing through?"

She shook her head. "He doesn't know details."

McManus looked at Mathis. "Whadaya think, Bob?"

"Show him the pictures and see how he reacts."

"What if he says he's never seen these people?" she said.

McManus said, "Then we know he's lying."

"Then what?"

An awkward silence.

Mathis said, "Okay, good point. Find out where Ramos lives. We could sit on it, see if this Sparrow character shows."

"Karen, we need that address," said McManus.

"I'll try. He told me he sleeps in his car sometimes. Other days, he said he stays at the safe house if Biggie needs him to run errands."

"Did he mention a woman?"

"Some kind of martial arts fanatic. Name's Tala. Her aunt owns more than one of these safe houses but Tala runs the place where Sparrow is staying."

"We've got to have that address, Karen. We could get a search warrant. Drop in on them and bag them both."

She folded her hands in front of her, her voice low. "You should know that Manny is genuinely afraid of the people he's working with."

"He should be," Mathis said. "Biggie Pacheco is the real deal. Bad people. This Sparrow guy sounds even scarier."

"Okay," McManus said, "if you think we've got something to work with, I'm on board with this." He turned to Mathis and raised an eyebrow.

"We should tail Ramos just to be sure," said Mathis.

"If he clams up about the safe house, can you keep him longer?" said Karen Little. "If I'm too obvious he'll shut down."

"Give it a try," said McManus. "Meanwhile, we'll get a tail set up. If he doesn't play ball, call Bob in and say, 'I think we're done here.' He can take off the cuffs and read him the riot act. You can play good cop, Karen."

Little returned to the interrogation room. In ten minutes, she called for Mathis. "I think we're done here," she said.

Mathis shrugged, stepped back into the hall, and called McManus. "We're gonna need the tail."

"You got it."

Mathis took his time before returning to the interview room. He made a show of removing the handcuffs. A suddenly energized Ramos, freed from the cuffs and cocky, confronted Mathis. "See, you had no right to do me like that. How about you give me a ride back?"

Mathis summoned his best scowl. "Whadaya think we're running here, a rapid transit station? Get the hell out of here. Next time there won't be a friendly probation officer to cut you loose. You owe her."

Ramos snorted at Mathis, then softened at Little. "Thanks, Miss Karen. I see you around, huh?"

"Stay out of trouble, Manny. I mean it. I can't always play this card."

"Doin' my best."

The two watched Ramos strut past the duty desk like a star.

Chapter 28

"We lost him?" McManus was not happy.

"Apparently Biggie Pacheco was there to pick Ramos up once we cut him loose," said Mathis. "Our guy spotted him getting into a SUV with Biggie. They got lost in traffic."

McManus slammed his fist, rattling the keyboard. "Dammit. Ramos was our lead to the safe house. Quick, make some calls. See if we can get some eyes in Mecca Town. We might get lucky."

"We should put a squad on that cellphone store," said Mathis. "He might go back there to get his car."

"How did Biggie know we had Ramos?"

"Maybe someone saw him get picked up. Coulda been someone on the way out when we brought Ramos in. A defense lawyer. I dunno. Take your pick."

McManus said, "This is not good, Bob. We have to nail this down tight. We still have the Sparrow out there."

Mathis said, "Have you considered that maybe Ramos was playing up this Sparrow guy as a heavyweight to get some attention?"

McManus shook his head. "No, Karen said he was genuinely scared of this guy. Have we run this woman's name through the system? Tala?"

"I put the word out to the gang unit. Haven't heard back yet."

McManus was dying for a cup of coffee. "Okay, keep me posted. This is top priority but it's not the only game in town right now."

Mathis paced, lost in thought.

"Do that somewhere else," said McManus. "You're distracting me."

"It's the coffee thing, isn't it?"

"I'm trying."

"Got it!"

"Got what?"

"Martial arts!"

"What the hell you talking about?"

Punching the air, Mathis brightened. "Martial arts. Didn't Ramos say this woman, Tala, was some sort of martial arts junkie?"

"Yeah, I do remember something like that."

"Bingo! She probably works out somewhere. They'd know her."

"Bob, how many *dojos* do you think we have in the city, county?"

Temporarily deflated, Mathis sulked. "Yeah. Maybe a thousand?"

McManus encouraged him. "Probably not that many. But start with those in Mecca Town. Work outward from there. Put together a list so we don't duplicate our search. I'll make some of those calls, too. If we get in over our heads we can get some of the gang guys who know that culture to help us."

Mathis sat in front of his computer, his fingers flying over the keyboard. "I'm on it." Staring at the screen, he said, "Tala, if you're out there, baby, show yourself."

While Mathis put together a list of *dojos*, gyms and martial arts training facilities, McManus put out a call for help from the department's street gang unit. "We're talking martial arts," he barked into the phone. "Most likely Asian stuff. Tae kwon do, karate, judo...do they do judo anymore? Filipino martial arts? I dunno, anything that covers that, okay? We're looking for a Filipino woman named Tala, last name unknown. Check the database, we posted some pictures of her and the guy she's been seen with. They're both persons of interest. If any of your guys know her name or where we should look, get back to us ASAP."

Mathis worked for an hour without success. McManus ran down his share of the list as well while keeping a finger on the pulse of the search for Ramos and Biggie Pacheco. Three hours went by with no hits and no sightings of Ramos.

McManus capitulated at the end of the day. He had a high school basketball game to attend along with his wife. His son was a starter. "Hate to desert you, Bob, but this game is a nonnegotiable for Laurie. I'll have my cell with me just in case."

Without looking up from his computer screen, Mathis sent him off with his blessing.

That evening, with his son's team down by six in the second half, McManus felt his phone vibrate. He kept his eyes on the court while listening to Mathis. One of the Asian gang detectives had called with good news. Late to the discussion because of an earlier bust, he told Mathis he remembered Tala.

"This guy sparred with her," said Mathis. "Said she's really good. A real dragon lady. Beautiful. Fast."

McManus said, "Great. Did he give you a last name?"

"No."

"Did he remember where she trained?"

"No. But he's checking with the meet's sponsor," said Mathis. "He'll call if he turns up anything."

"Okay, this is good work, Bob." Shifting in his bleacher seat, McManus put away the phone and rubbed his eyes with the heels of his hands.

"Good news?" his wife said.

"Yeah, that was Bob. We were due a break. She practically fell in our laps."

"Who?"

"A person of interest we've been trying to find."

"One of your endless collection of puzzle pieces?"

McManus groaned. His son had launched an air ball into the hands of an opponent. The mistake cost yet another basket. "That hurt," he said, pointing. "Teddy's head is not in the game."

"Like father, like son."

He groaned. "I'm here, Laurie."

"Your body is."

McManus didn't hear her sarcasm. He was back on the phone with Mathis. "Another thought, Bob. Follow up on Ramos. Somebody has to spot this guy. Make sure our patrols know how important he is. Biggie, too."

"They know, Mike. You're covered. Just enjoy the game."

"I'm trying but my kid's team is fading. Gotta go, Bob, I'm getting the look."

Chapter 29

American Embassy, Manila

Battling humidity, a stack of paperwork, and a headache, a weary John Stiles answered his office phone on the second ring.

"Yes, Maggie."

"Colonel Jose Rojas on line one."

"Is it necessary? Couldn't O'Connor take the call?"

"He's out. This falls in your lap. Take one for the team, John."

Groaning, Stiles said, "Ugh, fine, put him through."

Stiles, the embassy's "Legat"—short for legal attaché—was the FBI's eyes and ears in the Philippines. He grimaced, bracing himself for another one of Rojas's windy narratives. The colonel was an obsequious bureaucrat from the National Bureau of Investigation—NBI, the island nation's version of the FBI. Inherited from his predecessor, Rojas was a particular thorn in Stiles's side. Occasionally passing on credible reports of criminal wrongdoing, most of the colonel's calls were repetitive monologues about his stalled career and salacious gossip about the sloth of superiors.

Steeling himself for yet another round, Stiles ran a hand through his thinning brown hair, pushed his spectacles into place, and lied. "Colonel, good afternoon. To what do I owe the pleasure of your call?"

"Ah, Agent Stiles, how are you?"

"A little under the weather, Colonel. How may I help you?"

"The question is—how may I help you?"

This endless game, fumed Stiles. "Very well, Colonel, how might you help me?"

"We have a credible report of a professional assassin being hired to kill someone in your country. He may already be there."

Stiles pushed aside his paperwork and sat up, his attention piqued by Rojas's uncharacteristically blunt words. There was urgency in the officer's voice missing from previous calls.

"You have my undivided attention, sir."

"It would be better for us to meet in person."

Stiles groaned inwardly. *Can't we do this over the phone?* he thought. "I am rather at a disadvantage just now, Colonel. Unfortunately, the ambassador has given me the task of writing a briefing report for a congressional delegation."

"You have my sympathy," said Rojas. "I assure you, this wouldn't take long. It is of vital importance. You must hear me out."

"With all due respect, Colonel, couldn't it wait overnight?"

"Lives are at stake, Mr. Stiles."

Covering the receiver with his hand, Stiles sighed at his caller's ploy. "Very well, Colonel. Shall we meet at the usual spot?"

"Not this time. In the interest of time I will make it easy for you. Do you know the Lotus Garden Hotel where we first met?"

Stiles said, "Yes, on Padre Faura Street, correct?"

"Good. I am there now watching a rather interesting billiard match."

And likely nursing a tumbler of rum, thought Stiles. "Very well. I will catch a taxi and be there within ten minutes."

Rojas laughed. "You forget our traffic, Mr. Stiles. I will wait."

Stiles grabbed a notebook, told his secretary where he was going, and left for the hotel, his headache building. Just blocks away from the embassy on Roxas Boulevard, the small hotel was a favorite of the colonel for its modern but informal atmosphere.

Stiles suffered the capital's notorious gridlock and crossed the lobby's marble floors twenty minutes later. He found Rojas, in mufti, perched on a high stool in the glass-walled lounge. Glass in hand, the colonel was focused on the waning minutes of an ongoing billiard contest. He greeted Stiles, waved him into silence to watch a final, difficult shot, then ushered the FBI man to a corner table.

"You were right about the traffic, Colonel."

"A curse all *Manileños* know well. Ah, but to the business at hand."

"You were most insistent," said Stiles, eager to get to the point.

Rojas finished his rum and signaled for another. "Did you hear of the killing of JuJu Cruz yesterday?"

"All of the city heard of it. Hard to miss the news. A rather bold and bloody affair. Cruz was a particularly cruel character, was he not? A kingpin in Manila's underworld, true?"

"One of the worst." Rojas brooded, looking past Stiles to the deserted billiards table. "A most embarrassing episode for the government."

Stiles held his tongue as the server arrived with a fresh drink for Rojas. When she left, he said, "Embarrassing in what way, Colonel?"

"Already rumors of official complicity in Cruz's death are being repeated."

A nation of scandals, thought Stiles. *What's one more among so many?* "I'm sorry to hear that, Colonel. Is that an official confirmation?"

"Not yet. But it will be. Our police are riddled with miscreants."

"But also many brave men and women as well. Are you implying certain corrupt officers played a role in this man's death?"

The colonel sipped his rum. "This is strictly unofficial, of course."

Stiles nodded in complicit sympathy. "Of course."

"My sources say six uniformed officers arrested JuJu Cruz in Tondo on the pretext of taking him to meet with the national police commander. The fool went willingly."

"Alone?"

Another sip. "Only his lawyer accompanied him. A mistake on his part."

"I heard that both bodies were found."

"Yes. Executed and tossed in a canal among the other refuse."

"Have the murderers been arrested?"

"Murderer," corrected Rojas. "The information I have hints that one man did the shooting in a room where JuJu and his lawyer had been taken."

"One shooter?" said Stiles. "Interesting. Has he been picked up?"

Rojas snorted. "Would you expect him to be found out so soon?"

Manila's tabloids were filled with lurid stories of such summary executions on both sides of the aisle. Stiles had given up reading them months ago. The steady diet of such acts produced a callousness among those who read the numbing details. "Judging from past examples, I would guess not," said Stiles.

"You would be correct," said Rojas. "Oh, there may be some of the guilty collared for show. Those who order such things will go unpunished. No one will lament the death of JuJu Cruz."

Stiles sagged, hoping for the conversation to lead somewhere, anywhere. "You spoke of an assassin in my country. Am I right to surmise there is a connection with your warning and the death of Cruz, Colonel? It's not exactly clear to me, sir. You have been forthright with me on past occasions. I'm, of course, eager to hear your thoughts on this threat to my nation."

"Ah, yes. The connection." Rojas finished his rum and nodded conspiratorially. "I can tell you this. Several weeks ago there was a meeting of criminal bosses in Tondo chaired by the late JuJu Cruz. At this gathering a request was made by one of the participants, we don't know which one, asking the others to recommend a professional killer for hire. This criminal was to travel to your country to fulfill his mission."

"Your sources are impressive." Stiles snagged a pen and jotted notes as Rojas talked. "Please go on, Colonel," he encouraged.

"The man hired is known only to us as *Ang Maya*—the Sparrow. He is most professional. He has murdered quite a few people. That much we know. He is extremely dangerous."

"Obviously. Do you perhaps know his target in America?"

Ignoring the question, Rojas said instead, "He is the one who we believe killed JuJu Cruz. You see the irony, Agent Stiles?"

"Forgive me, Colonel," Stiles said, "but if you mean the irony of JuJu Cruz arranging this killer's mission only to be murdered himself by this same man, then yes, I would find that ironic indeed."

Rojas licked at drops of rum on the tumbler's rim. "Some would call it justice."

Trying to hide his exasperation, Stiles repeated his question. "Do you know his target in America?"

"A person or persons in California is the best we can deduce at this time."

"No formal name for either the assassin or the victim?"

"Correct."

"Do you have a city in California in mind, perhaps?"

"Regrettably, no."

"Can you pinpoint the time he was hired, or perhaps when he left your country for mine?"

"We believe he fled only yesterday."

"The timing seems odd, sir, does it not? When you called earlier you said the killer might already be in America."

"Did I say that?" Pursing his lips, Rojas said, "Perhaps I was mistaken."

Stiles steamed silently. "I have to ask, sir. If his plan was known, why wasn't he arrested before he left the country?"

Rojas parsed the question. "He had help. That much is obvious."

"It would seem so. Is the killer's nickname significant?"

"Do you know our recent history, Agent Stiles?"

"I confess I am deficient in that, sir."

"A shame," scolded Rojas. "You Americans. You are not the only one."

Stiles stifled his resentment as the colonel took on a professorial tone. "There was a band of criminals in the eighties, communists, of course. One of many groups that plagued our country. They were the New People's Army. Their urban arm was known as the Alex Boncayao Brigade."

"After their fallen leader, correct?"

Rojas brightened. "Ah, so you do know this particular history."

"I've read about it but that was some time ago. Please continue."

"They targeted many of our people, foreigners as well. This group gathered about them assassins. Small in number, they were secretive and deadly." Rojas stabbed a finger at the table. "They were called sparrows, you see. They killed several of our officials. Also one of your countryman working in your embassy, Colonel James Rowe, in 1989. A most brazen attack on an American hero from your war in Vietnam. It was a shameful act. Once a captive of the Viet Cong, Colonel Rowe escaped his jungle prison only to die at the hands of criminals. These murders continued for some time before we were able to capture or kill these people." Rojas threw up his hands. "Extreme measures were taken. Much money changed hands. Unfortunately, much blood was spilled."

"It often is to root out evil," said Stiles. "And this professional killer. Is he connected somehow?"

"Unknown. He took the name of those killers from years past, perhaps for a reason. Perhaps to mislead us." The colonel ordered yet another rum.

"Is it at all possible to uncover his identity?" pressed Stiles. "Maybe a link, something my superiors can use to search for this man? It would be most helpful."

"Too long ago, I think. However, if we learn more I will call you."

"I certainly hope so, Colonel. I am most appreciative of this warning. I will alert our government immediately."

Armed with a fresh drink, Rojas warmed to his subject. "If only others in the government were as vigilant as myself we would have more to work with. Sometimes information such as this is ignored. Some of our senior officers are not like-minded, they do not realize the gravity of the situation. I have often said..."

Not now, thought Stiles. "Colonel Rojas, if I may. Might we continue this conversation at a future time? Time is of the essence. Unlike those in your ranks who are slow to realize the danger, you of all people must appreciate my situation. I must contact my superiors at once."

"I understand. We are of one mind, you and I. Yes, do what you must."

"Our government owes you a debt, sir. I commend you for bringing this to my attention. I'll pass this on to the ambassador and the bureau's director."

"We shall talk again," said Rojas.

"Indeed we shall, Colonel. Please excuse me."

"Yes, of course."

"Goodbye."

"Dodged a bullet," said Stiles aloud when he reached the street and hailed a taxi. "Now to make sure the killer's target, whoever that is, dodges one as well."

His headache suddenly gone, Stiles returned to his office and began typing an "Information Only" email to the Bureau's Washington field office.

"Friendly sources here alerted us today..."

He deleted the text, tried again.

"Sources in the National Bureau of Investigation..."

Deleted.

"My confidential sources confided in me
within the past hour..."

Much better. Pointing out where credit was due.

Finishing the message, he reread it, tightened it, and,
pleased with the result, hit send. It was a good effort but
if Rojas was correct, the killer had a head start.

Chapter 30

McManus filled his office doorway with a large coffee, a
bad start to the day. Mathis followed him in, adding to his
misery. "How did your son's game turn out?"

"Lousy. He and another kid tied for team goat."

"There will always be a next time."

"Not at this pace." McManus settled behind his desk with
his coffee. "Tell me something to cheer me up."

"Still waiting for word on where this Tala trained."

"That's not helping. Any word of the whereabouts of
Ramos?"

Mathis rocked on the balls of his feet. "Still looking."

"We should talk to Biggie."

"Looking for him as well."

Scowling, McManus rubbed his forehead. "Damn, the
city can't suddenly be that big."

To add to McManus's woes, another detective showed,
rapping knuckles on the doorframe impatiently. "The captain
wants a word, Mike."

"Be right there." Grumbling, McManus heaved himself
from his chair. "Probably gonna get my ass chewed for this
mess we're in."

Mathis held up his hands. "They didn't hear it from
me, Mike."

"We had so many feelers out there it was bound to leak."

"I'll make some calls while you're with the assistant principal."

Mathis started working the phones.

McManus trudged down the hall, knocked. "You wanted to see me, Captain?"

"Yeah, Mike. Come in, have a seat."

"If it's about this case we're working on..."

The captain, a gruff desk jockey with steel gray hair and intimidating stare, ignored the comment and tapped his computer screen. "Not sure it's connected. Just got off the phone with the feds. Special Agent Bryson called to ruin my day. You know, sometimes I think he enjoys doing that." He swiveled in his chair to face McManus. "The Bureau got an alert from their man in Manila. Now Homeland Security's going nuts. Seems we might have an assassin on the loose somewhere in the state."

McManus nodded, saying nothing.

Hunched over his desk, the captain folded his arms, his eyes shifting from McManus to his computer screen and back again. "They didn't specify which city, only that California was thought to be where this guy was headed. They're looking at Sacramento, San Francisco, LA or us. The feds say this is solid intel coming from some source in Filipino law enforcement...which is a contradiction in my book, by the way."

Turning from McManus, the captain stared at his monitor and read aloud.

"'For information of receiving offices: Legat, Manila was advised by the NBI that information from an undisclosed source of undisclosed reliability indicates a professional killer known only as Sparrow—no descriptive data available—has been hired by an unknown individual in the Philippines to kill an unknown individual, or individuals, in the United States— likely California—for reasons not known to the NBI.'"

He arched an eyebrow at McManus. "How's that for nailing it down for you?"

McManus sat on the edge of his chair, excitement in his voice. "Sparrow. That's it. Sir, that's the name we have for the guy who showed up last week on a flight from Honolulu. We've been tracking this guy."

Arms behind his head, the captain leaned back, pointing to his monitor. "But according to the bureau's warning, the timing's all wrong, Detective. They say he left twenty-four hours ago, maybe forty-eight at the most."

"What about the name, Captain? That's no coincidence. I'm willing to gamble it's the same guy."

"Okay, I'll give you the name, but the timing is all off."

McManus got to his feet to peer at the screen. "I grant you that it's not exactly a clear picture, sir. But we have a name, probably an alias, and several sightings."

A groan from behind the desk. "The same guy can't be in two places at the same time."

McManus poked a finger at the screen. "My gut says it's the same guy."

"For sake of an argument let's say you're right. What's this alert mean for the status of your investigation?"

Hands on hips, McManus said, "Mathis and I have been on this since the Harbor Patrol spotted our suspect being picked up at the airport."

"One Ramon Reyes. Yeah, I read the preliminary report. Did you check on the Honolulu end?"

"Nothing."

"So where did this person go?"

"We have reason to believe he went to ground in a safe house run by Biggie Pacheco. We're guessing it's somewhere in Mecca Town."

"Because...?"

"Because we picked up one of the gangbangers who met this guy at the airport. We talked to him, got some useful stuff, and let him go, hoping he'd lead us to the safe house."

"But your tail lost him, correct?"

McManus deflated. "Bad news travels fast. He skipped, but we'll find him."

"I assume you have the word out on the street."

McManus nodded. "Covered like a blanket."

"I hear there's a woman involved, right? What's the skinny on that?"

"We're pursuing leads on her as well."

"Pretty slim pickings, Mike." The captain lumbered to his feet, a signal the meeting was over. "Okay, keep me posted. If you want more resources, ask. If you're right about this guy being the same man the feds are worried about you'll need help."

McManus said, "I'm betting the feds are casting a wide net. This probably falls in the terrorist category."

"Yeah, they've alerted ATF, Homeland Security, and ICE. They're spread thin, won't put any resources into your case until they're one hundred percent sure this is the same guy. Meanwhile, we've got a three-ring circus going on between what the Filipinos are telling us, the feds, and what we know for sure."

"The more the merrier, I'd say."

"So we're looking for one guy."

"Sparrow. That's my bet."

The captain growled. "Nail his ass. Make the collar, Mike."

"Will do." McManus paused in the doorway. "One more thing, sir. You should know the guy we're looking for is the same one who showed up on Sam McFadden's doorstep and visited his gun range."

"McFadden? What's he got to do with this?"

"That's the missing piece. He's as mystified as we are."

"We talking about the same guy?"

"Positive sighting both times, sir."

"You think McFadden could be the target?"

McManus shrugged.

"Wait a minute, Mike. Isn't McFadden's wife Filipino?"

"Part Filipino, sir. On her dad's side."

The captain snapped his fingers. "Yeah, that could be it. Better talk to Sam and his wife. I forget her name."

"Reggie."

"Yeah. Her father was some Pooh-Bah in the armed forces there. Wasn't there some dustup with him, some gangsters? You know, something about McFadden starting a business in the islands?"

"Good memory. Yeah, Sam and his wife had to get out of Dodge."

"The whole thing ended badly, correct?"

"I believe so, sir. McFadden's friend Tom Wolf was part of that."

"The retired Navy SEAL?"

"The same."

The captain's shaggy brow furrowed. "All that fiasco with the Russian mob two years ago. McFadden and Wolf, right?"

"That's right."

"Geez, that's all we need. Wolf was a bit of a loose cannon, wasn't he?"

"Kind of a wild man, but in a good sense, sir. He had McFadden's back."

"Word to the wise, Mike. Do not let this get out of hand. We don't need a repeat of what happened. If this is as far as your operation has gone so far, beware. With the feds sniffing around I'm gonna need to cover my ass on this. I don't want any surprises. Neither does the chief."

"Understood."

"Good. Talk with McFadden and his wife. They might be able to tell you more about why they're possible targets. I'll get the feds in on it if they're interested. Whadaya think?"

"Makes sense."

"Don't blow smoke up my ass, Mike."

"No, sir. It would put us all on the same page."

"Okay, get moving. Make the calls. I'll back you with whatever you need to get a handle on this."

"Appreciate it."

Energized by the conversation, McManus hurried back to brief Mathis but found his office empty. A yellow note was stuck on his computer screen:

Mike,
Arnie Ige from Western Division called. Body found DOA this AM. Couple on Ocean Beach bike path spotted body in San Diego River near Smiley Lagoon. Initial reports sound like Ramos—tattoos, etc. Headed there to confirm ID. Will call. ME on scene. Better bag Biggie ASAP.
Mathis

Chapter 31

Pulled in from the patio by a panicked Biggie Pacheco, Tala, still in a robe, her hair damp, stared at him. "What's happened?"

Biggie drew blinds across the glass doors. "We have to leave immediately!"

"Why?"

"Manny."

Hearing the commotion, Sparrow came out of his room. "What about him?"

"He was picked up yesterday. Cops took him downtown."

Tala grabbed Biggie's arm. "How'd you find out?"

Biggie paced in a tight circle, eyes on the floor. "Got a call from one of the brothers at the cellphone shop. He said a detective named Mathis was running the show out there. This guy had a squad grab Manny. Another brother downtown saw him going inside with two cops.

Sparrow remained calm. "But why do we have to leave?"

As if explaining to a slow child, Biggie said, "Because he was in there for hours, *manong*. What you think they talked about?"

Feeling Biggie's alarm, Tala demanded, "Where's Manny now?"

Pacheco ignored the question, saying instead, "We got to get you both to another place. Maybe Manny said something. Maybe he let something slip about this place. Can't risk it. They probably looking for us. Got to go now."

"I have to call my auntie," said Tala. "She'll need to know."

"No good. Cops picked up your auntie half hour ago."

"What?"

"Actually, she turned herself in. She called me to give a warning, eh."

"Why would she do that?" fumed Tala. "You're lying."

"Hey, no offense, but she said she was gonna tell them she got no idea what you doing with her house. Her story makes sense if she wanna save her ass. This house busted now anyway. Got to leave."

"She'd never do that," challenged Tala. "We're family."

"You don't get it, Tala," barked an anxious Biggie Pacheco. "She can say you running this scam on her. Like she didn't know nothing 'bout what was going on."

"Harboring a fugitive is a problem, Tala," he added. "I make a risk myself coming over here to warn you. I gotta stay low, too."

Her mind racing, Tala saw disaster threatening.

"Perhaps Biggie's right," said Sparrow. "Everything is lost if police show up."

"Where are we going?" she said.

"I have the van outside," Biggie said. "Grab what you need. I take you to another place. You be safe there, but hurry."

Gathering what little he had, Sparrow helped Tala carry her belongings to the idling van in the carport. Biggie locked the doors and climbed behind the wheel. "Lay down on the seats," he ordered. "Even with tinted windows, better nobody see you leaving."

Suspicion in her voice, Tala said, "Is this really necessary?"

"Do it," said Biggie. "Take no chances."

When they had driven for ten minutes, Biggie told them they could sit up. Neither did. Tala fought rising panic as they drove for another fifteen minutes through winding neighborhood streets. In the seat behind her, Sparrow stayed hidden as well. When the van slowed, then stopped, they sat upright.

Biggie had pulled into the driveway of a rambler set back from the street. Overgrown bushes lined a driveway of broken asphalt. The new refuge's weedy front lawn had recently been badly mowed. Given the reason for their flight the hideaway would have to do. Only when the engine stopped did Biggie relax.

Parked under a sagging carport, he said, "Wait here. I goin' check the house to make sure." He came back within minutes and ushered them inside.

The home's interior was stuffy, dark; the carpet, soiled beige. He had pulled heavy drapes across an enormous picture window in a room at the front of the house. Two bedrooms and a single bathroom, a galley kitchen, and a breakfast area paved in curling linoleum took up the first floor. The furniture was old, smelling faintly of mold. Beyond the drawn curtains, a tiny backyard of thirsty grass fenced by tall, thick hedges offered what they needed most—privacy.

"Okay, I make a store run for you. After that I have to disappear, eh?"

Arms folded, Tala blocked the side door to the carport. "How long are we going to be here?"

Biggie sighed. "No idea. I get my boys to come over later. If the cops don't show in the next couple days we be okay."

"And if the police show?" she said.

Another resigned sigh. "Then we got big problems."

Biggie tossed a prepaid cellphone to Tala and scribbled a number on a scrap of paper. "If you need me, call. You see something not right, call."

He peeked out the front window's drapes. "Got to go. Remember, don't let nobody inside 'cept our people."

Tala grabbed Biggie's arm. "Where you going?"

"Things a little hot right now, eh? I got to disappear."

"You can't leave us here," she said, tightening her grip. "We have no way to get around. We can't leave."

"Just for now," he said. Prying her fingers from his arm, he said, "Stay out of sight. You good for now."

"I send some food, eh? Just before dawn. Keep an eye out for my boy."

He was out the door and in the van before Sparrow could stop him.

Silent, arms folded, Tala sat in one of the room's overstuffed chairs. When Biggie left, Sparrow pulled a bottle of water from his bag and offered it. She took it, sipping slowly, her mind focused on the situation. Sparrow explored every room and returned to pace in front of the drawn curtains. Tala turned on a weak lamp beside her on an end table.

"Don't do that," he commanded.

Scowling, she turned it off. "Don't you think a dark house will attract more attention?"

Yielding, Sparrow said. "You're right. Maybe just the one light."

She turned it on again and fell silent.

"I'm sorry to have brought you into this," he said.

Tearful, she said, "Things have not turned out as I hoped."

"I will make McFadden pay for this," he said.

Chapter 32

In the pre-dawn, Tala awakened to the sound of low voices coming from the kitchen. The rich aroma of coffee drew her. The unexpected early morning visit had interrupted Sparrow's ritual cleaning of his handgun. On the tiny table an oily rag with two loaded twelve-round magazines shared space with remnants of a meager breakfast of peanut butter and bread. Across from Sparrow sat a man she had seen before. One of Biggie's gang associates, he looked familiar but she had forgotten his name.

Sparrow smiled. "Tala, this is Cesar," he said, "Biggie sent him with food."

Their visitor showed a crooked smile full of bad teeth. "Hey, Tala."

She nodded without speaking, taking in the greasy hair, scraggly goatee, and brown pockmarked face— Cesar. His voice a clue, she placed him. A slippery felon with a reputation with the ladies. She had once raked his clumsy paw with her talons at a party. Tala still remembered the drunken affront even if Cesar didn't.

"Where's Biggie?" she demanded.

"Out of sight...for now. Staying low. He sent me. Things hot, you know?"

Cesar grinned, his eyes on Tala. "Biggie, a man of his word. He also sent beer and ice cream. I already put it away for you."

Tala snorted. "Beer and ice cream. How thoughtful."

"Better eat something," Sparrow said to her, waving the Beretta.

Famished, Tala toasted a piece of bread, spread it with peanut butter, and devoured it. She fixed another slice, washed it down with orange juice in a paper cup, and wandered to a window. The dawn sky was a deep gray, low clouds with a teasing hint of rain for a thirsty city. She stood with her back to the men, feeling Cesar's eyes undressing her. Tala poured a cup of coffee, dumped in sugar, and stirred it with a plastic spoon.

"Where's Manny?" she asked. "Cops still have him?"

"Nobody's seen him," said Cesar.

She stared at him and got a shrug as if he didn't know or care.

"What's Biggie think?"

The same disinterested shrug.

Sparrow put his handgun together and slapped a magazine in the Beretta. He jacked a round in the chamber and sighted the muzzle at the ceiling. "Tell her what you do know, Cesar."

Their visitor glanced at Sparrow. "You sure, *manong*?"

"Of course, she deserves to hear it."

Curiosity aroused, she challenged him. "What do you know, Cesar?"

Slouching in his chair, Biggie's envoy said, "Your picture's all over the news." He nodded at Sparrow. "Both of you. Persons of interest, the cops saying."

Tala scowled at the news. Sparrow was unmoved.

"Your auntie made bail, Tala." Cesar got up from the table. "Okay, next stop, I got to see Biggie. He's working on a plan.

I think maybe you two and him going over the border for a while. Maybe to Arizona."

"I have one thing to do before I can go away," said Sparrow.

Cesar paused at the door to the carport. "What you have to do?"

"Just tell Biggie I need one, maybe two, more days."

"I don't think he'll like this idea, *manong*."

Sparrow turned the Beretta in his hand, his eyes on the pistol, not Cesar. "He'll understand. Tell him."

"Okay. Your funeral. He won't be happy."

"Tell him."

With Cesar gone, Sparrow wrapped the weapon in the rag. He reached for Tala's hand. "Do you believe me when I say that once McFadden is dead I will be done with this business?"

"I don't know. So much has happened in these last days...since..."

"Since you came to my room that night?"

"Don't confuse what you are going to do with what happened."

"I know it had nothing to do with what I must do now."

"But that's what I don't understand. Why go through with this?"

"Something I have to do," he said. "I will have a future when this is done."

"If you are successful."

"I have never failed. Not once. The man who sent me does not tolerate failure. I gave him my word I would not fail, Tala."

"The police will be expecting you. They also looking for me..."

"I know. I have a plan. You good with a razor?"

Puzzled, she said, "If you mean like, in a fight, yes."

"Not like that. Like cutting hair."

"I guess so. Why you ask?"

He ran a hand through his thick black hair. "I need you to make me look older. *Mantanda*—you know, like an old man. Can you do this?"

"You sure?"

"Yes. It will help. I will no longer be the wanted man in the pictures."

"Ah, I see what you mean." For the first time in days a light flashed in her eyes. She smiled. "Okay, I have a razor in my bag. Trust me. You can see in the mirror if you like what I do."

"Do what you wish. I'm sure it will be fine."

She had him sit on a stool in the kitchen, wrapped a towel around his shoulders, and began cutting. She combed, cut again, and nipped at loose strands with her razor until satisfied. She added touches of eyebrow pencil under his eyes. When finished, Tala marched him before the cracked bathroom mirror. Even in the weak light of a forty-watt bulb over the sink, the transformation was dramatic.

"Oh, this is good," he purred. "Better than I thought it could be."

Sparrow's youthful look had been exchanged for that of an elder three times his age. "Now," he said. "We have only to ask Cesar to bring me some old clothes. Let the police look for a man who does not exist, eh?"

"I know," she said, "a *multo*. An invisible spirit."

Staring at the reflection, he took Tala's hands in his. "A spirit who kills."

She let the comment pass. "But what about me?" she said, fingering her luxurious locks.

"We cut your hair short," he said, reaching for the razor. "Put lots of powder on it, get you some glasses. You can look old, no problem."

Glancing from Sparrow's reflection to her own, Tala said, "Maybe. It could work. Only one thing, I cut my own hair, not you."

"Good. No one looking for a gardener and an old woman, eh?"

Chapter 33

Ocean Beach

Detective Bob Mathis cut through the town's north end and turned onto Bacon Street, aiming for the San Diego River channel. The road curved to the right, bisecting baseball diamonds belonging to Robb Field. A rowdy group of ultimate frisbee fanatics surged across a field on his left. He passed three couples harnessed to labs headed to Dog Beach. He parked alongside two squad cars in the lot. A medical examiner's van had backed diagonally across two spots. Two officers were doing crowd control at the lot's entrance, two more along the paved river pathway where cyclists and the curious had gathered.

Mathis got out of the car; the detective's badge on the chain around his neck and the holstered pistol on one hip got him through the perimeter. He headed to the water where a huddle of cops kibitzed on a sloping bank of a downstream branch. The sluggish tributary fed Smiley Lagoon.

Recognizing Detective Arne Ige in the distance, Mathis waved. When he arrived, he shook hands with the men. After small talk, Ige and two detectives walked him to the body, which lay face up, clad only in undershorts.

Ige said, "One of yours, right, Bob?"

Mathis stared down at the corpse aground on the rocks. "Manny Ramos."

The two detectives overheard him. One said, "You know him?"

Turning to the pair, Mathis sighed. "Manny Ramos. A person of interest in a case we're working."

"You're positive on the ID?"

Tilting his head to study the face, Mathis nodded. "Yeah, it's him. Tattoos match. Face is still pretty much recognizable. It's him."

The other cop said, "Gangbanger?"

"Oh yeah, that he is. Thanks for the call, Arnie. Manny Ramos. He's in the system."

Ige said, "Thanks. That'll save us some legwork." He said something to the two detectives and sent them away. He and Mathis stared down at the corpse's battered face as if studying a broken brown vase.

Squatting, Mathis peered at the body. "What's the medical examiner say?" Chin in hand, Ige said, "First pass says your boy was strangled. Pretty obvious. Ligature marks always a red flag."

Mathis pointed with a pen. "Notice the burn marks on the torso and arms?"

"Cigarette burns," said Ige. "Whoever did this took their time."

"Probably looking for the same information we were."

Mathis looked upstream. A pair of crime scene techs in waders were dutifully probing the river's shallows on either side with poles. Ige followed his gaze. "We're still looking for clothing, anything connected. Nothing so far."

Scanning the Sunset Cliffs Boulevard Bridge, Mathis pointed. "Think he might have been tossed from there?"

"Can't say for certain. Maybe. Easier to stop along the bike path and hustle him over here where he'd be found."

"Huh," said Mathis. "I dunno, Arnie. Late at night. Alone on the bridge. Slow down, pull to the side, and over he goes. Nothing to it."

"You could be right. I'm not going to second-guess you."

Mathis tugged on his right ear, eyes still on the bridge. "It's just that it's the first time I've seen one of our wayward citizens dumped here. Not much of a statement to have him end up near Smiley Cove."

"True. Shocked the hell out of two bikers this morning, though."

"Not the best way to start your day," said Mathis.

"I'm sure your victim would agree."

Mathis shook his head. "A shame. We had our hands on him not more than forty-eight hours ago. Sad. Didn't need to be."

"Amen. You're preaching to the choir, Bob." Ige backed away. "We've got our pictures. Swept the scene. If you have no objections we'll bag him."

"Your call, Arnie. I need to phone McManus. This might send us back to square one."

"Let me know if you need anything else."

They shook hands. Mathis turned away from the body, his eyes on a small knot of gawkers lining the bikeway. He knew Ige's people would likely have already talked to potential witnesses but he made a mental note to double-check. He trudged across rocks and weeds lining the riverbank and called McManus to tell him one of their puzzle pieces had turned up.

Chapter 34

A fire-engine red Harley Roadster and ebony Softail arrived in McFadden's driveway belching trademark thunder. Drawn by the roar, Reggie pried apart the blinds at a bay window, took one look, and called Wolf to her side. The bikers, hulking, bandana-wearing graybeards with ponytails and leathers, dismounted and ambled to the front porch. The taller of the two rang the doorbell. A reluctant Reggie sent Wolf in her place. He opened the door, his shoulder wedged behind it as a precaution.

"Afternoon, gentlemen, what can I do for you?"

"Looking for Tom Wolf."

"Who's asking?"

"Friends. I'm Roderick, this here's Duke. You Wolf?"

Wolf said, "Define 'friends' for me."

Roderick planted a boot on the stone threshold and gave Wolf a business card.

He scanned the name. "Walt Jonski. Sure, the Marine at the restaurant bar."

Wolf handed back the card. "Why the house call? Walt doing okay?"

"Not at present," said Roderick, the bigger man.

Duke, the second biker, spoke. "That's why we're here, Commander. He just got out of the hospital yesterday."

"Hospital? What happened, bike accident?"

"Payback."

Puzzled, Wolf stepped over the threshold. "Explain that to me."

"Those guys you and Walt took out at that restaurant."

"They put him in the hospital?"

Roderick, the Softail's owner, shifted his weight. "They tracked him down and paid a visit. Beat the shit out of him, broke a leg, and roughed up his old lady."

"Why? He didn't press charges for the bar fight even though they started it."

"That's Walt for you," said Duke.

"I'm sorry to hear this. He call the cops about this latest confrontation?"

Duke said, "Not Walt's thing. Though he did ask us to stop by and see if you'd be willing to help dispense a little justice."

Rubbing his jaw, Wolf glanced over his shoulder at a worried Reggie. He turned to the bikers. "Let's take this conversation to the driveway, okay?"

The three walked to the parked motorcycles. Wolf started with small talk. He ran his hands over the Roadster's lines and tooled leather seat. "Beautiful bike."

"That's mine," said Duke. "You ride, sir?"

"It's Tom, not 'sir' these days," said Wolf. "And no, Duke, sorry to say, I don't ride anymore. Always liked the look of this bike. No offense, Roderick, Softails are wicked machines but Roadsters have my heart."

The three laughed.

"Uh, about Walt," said Roderick. "So, whadaya think?"

"My first thought would be to call the cops. Press charges."

"Walt thought a shortcut might be in order," said Duke.

"I hear you," said Wolf, "but it's risky." He snapped his fingers. "You pay a visit to these guys and the next thing you know, everything goes south."

"We figure to mount up a dozen guys," said Roderick. "Keep things low-key."

"Twelve bikers is hardly low-key," said Wolf.

Duke folded his arms, feet spread in a martial pose, his dark eyebrows knitted in a frown. "Walt said you were a SEAL, sir...Tom."

"I was," said Wolf, circling the bikes. "I was young and foolish then."

"Walt said you can still kick ass."

"We did that night. He was right there to help."

"Now he needs your help," said Roderick. "We're just thinking a serious ass whooping to put an end to this tit-for-tat shit."

"Yeah," said Duke. "Show the colors. You could be, you know, a force multiplier like they say."

Wolf cocked his head, said, "Your guys are all vets, right?"

"Marines. Semper Fi!" both chorused.

Roderick said, "Duke drove H-34's. I was his crew chief."

Wolf smiled. "Nice to stay together after all those years."

"Roger that," said Duke. "So, about Walt's problem..."

Intrigued, Wolf played with the Softail's throttle, his eyes locked on Roderick. "What's your plan? There were three guys, you know."

"We're going after the big dawg," said Roderick. "He's the one who broke Walt's leg."

"The phony SEAL," said Wolf, kneeling to eyeball the Softail's engine. He looked up at Roderick. "I remember him. Loud. Cocky. Drunk."

"Name's Sheldon Dix," said Duke, shaking his head. "Guy never served a day. We know where this asshole lives." He leaned across the Roadster's seat. "It's Dix we want. He's the brains of this operation, if you can call him that."

"And the plan?" said a skeptical Wolf, standing. "You just going to break down the guy's door and jump him? What about a wife, kids."

Duke warmed to the subject. "We've done two recons, Skipper. Dix lives alone. We thought we'd stop over with enough guys to make him shit his pants. We're willing to step on him to make our point if we have to."

Wolf stood up, mounted the Softail, getting a feel for bike, both feet on the ground. "What if he's packing? Thought of that?" Waiting for an answer, his gaze fell on the instrument dials.

"We'll risk it," boasted Roderick. "Knock on the door. Go in fast."

"Kinda crazy if you ask me," said Wolf. "I mean, showing up with twelve guys on bikes is overkill."

"What's wrong with numbers like that?"

"You lose the element of surprise for one thing. You don't sneak up on a guy riding hogs."

That stopped them cold. "What do you suggest?" said Duke.

"A night visit."

"Huh, I see your point," said Duke.

"You take three, maybe four guys at most." Wolf got off the Harley. "What you lose in numbers you make up for in surprise." He made a fist. "You're tighter. Less worry about one of your guys doing something stupid."

A light went on in Roderick's eyes. "Yeah, I get it. Trying to handle too many guys is like..." He waved his hands, searching for words. "Like herding cats,"

"Exactly," said Wolf, arms folded. "This is your project, gentlemen. I don't mean to horn in on your necktie party."

"No, no, this is good," said Roderick. "That's why Walt said to talk to you."

"So, what would you do?" said Duke, scratching his head.

"I'd go in at night. I'd go with four guys, max. I'd go unarmed, no guns. And I'd go with gloves, ski masks or bandanas. No need to let Dix know who you are."

Clapping his hands, Duke said, "I like it. Get in, get his attention, deliver our message, get out."

Roderick was sold. Rubbing his hands, he said, "I'm in. When can we do it?"

"Yeah, and will you go with us?" said Duke.

Wolf paused, chin in hand. "Look, if I agree to do this I need a return favor."

"Damn. Ask and ye shall receive," said a grinning Roderick.

"Here's the deal, gentlemen." Wolf gestured to McFadden's house. "I'm in a jam here. Sort of housebound. I'd need some short-term protection for my friend and his wife. They're good people. I'm thinking maybe one or two guys like yourselves hanging around here as watchdogs day and night for a couple weeks, no more."

"Scare the kids and keep the neighbors away kind of thing?" said Duke.

"For show, but it might get a little heavier than that."

Duke leaned on the Roadster's tank, his eyes on Wolf. "What's going on that you need to babysit your friends?"

Wolf sketched a brief outline about the FBI warnings and the loose assassin.

Fascinated by the telling, both agreed to commit their group in return for Wolf's help. If he would pay a visit to Walt Jonski's assailant in company with the Marine veterans, they'd provide security for the McFaddens.

"Done," Wolf said, shaking hands with the two. "I'll want to talk to Walt."

"Aye, aye, sir," boomed Roderick. "He was expecting your call either way."

"It's Tom," Wolf corrected him, "or I'll answer to Wolfman."

"Roger that, sir. Old habits die hard," said Roderick, grinning as he said it.

"And I'd need to do my own recon drive-by on Dix's place. The sooner the better. One bike with me on the back so we don't attract a lot of attention."

"Done," said Roderick, straddling the Softail, boots planted on the concrete. "We can go now if you'd like. Ride with me."

Glancing across the driveway at the front door, Wolf thumbed over his shoulder, saying, "I'll alert the lady of the house that you two are harmless and that I'm just going for a ride."

Drawing himself to his full height, Roderick barked, "Harmless. That's a helluva insult."

Wolf shrugged, hands jammed in his jeans. "Duke, can you stand fast while we're gone?"

"Will do."

Wolf disappeared into the house, explained the situation to Reggie, and came outside wearing a dark green windbreaker.

She walked to the doorway, waved as Wolf introduced the two, and then went back inside.

Wreathed in blue fumes, Roderick sat on his idling bike as Wolf climbed aboard. He said, "Back within the hour, Duke."

They rode away, the big Softail shattering the neighborhood's serenity.

Chapter 35

Tala returned to the chair in the front room. Sparrow foraged in the drawers, inventorying plastic forks and spoons, pots and pans, and a set of kitchen knives.

"What are you going to do," said Tala, leaning against the doorframe, "go after your man with that instead of your pistol?"

Sparrow twirled the largest knife in his hand. "I have done it before. If this was all I had to work with, I could do it again."

"I don't want to be part of this."

Sparrow pointed the heavy blade at her. "I know. But do not forget, Tala, we have been seen together."

"Yes, but we were doing nothing illegal. I have nothing to fear from the police."

He took a step toward her. "I think you underestimate their willingness to punish anyone involved with me."

Tala eyed the blade and pistol in his waistband. "You mean to threaten me?"

"Why would I do that? You have helped me. You have risked much to shelter me. You faced McFadden with me. I am only pointing out the obvious."

"I asked you before," she said. "Why pursue this when you have been abandoned by the people who hired you to kill McFadden? I'm the one who found him for you. They did not. I went with you on both occasions. They did not.

They did nothing but send you on a hopeless mission. Abandon this madness while there's still time. We could go away together."

"Don't try to confuse me, Tala. I know what I am to do. The fact that I have to search on my own sometimes is part of what I do. And I am paid well for this."

"What good is money? We are on the run, stuck in this ugly house, dependent on others for our safety. It is only a matter of time before the police find us. What then?"

"I will disappear."

She laughed. "Here we call that believing your own press."

"This is not the time for doubt," he said. "This is the time to think, to plan, to stay one step ahead of your pursuers. I have always done this."

Tala swept her arm around the room. "Plan? Do you see where we are? We are prisoners. We wait on Biggie. We can't breathe this way."

"You want to leave?"

"Of course. We could both leave this behind. Go while we still can."

Sparrow put away the knife and retreated to the living room's oppressive gloom, pistol in hand. He sank into a chair and stared at the floor. Tala followed him, sitting opposite. They sat without speaking for two hours. She drifted off, awoke, fell asleep again. Traffic on the street was sporadic. Somewhere a dog barked until hoarse. A car alarm went off, was silenced, started again.

The day dragged on, changing to afternoon. Sparrow opened a window.

"Are you hungry?" he finally asked.

"I don't feel like eating."

"I will make something," he said. "Will you join me?"

She didn't answer.

Sparrow went into the kitchen. She heard him rummage in the refrigerator, then drag a chair across the linoleum to sit at the table. Eating was the last thing on her mind. Cornered, dispirited, she crawled onto a naked mattress in one of the bedrooms and tried to sleep. She heard Sparrow wandering about the house. On one of his vigils he stopped in the doorway. She pretended to sleep, her eyelids barely closed, watching him. He backed from the room and continued his rounds.

Eventually, she drifted off.

Chapter 36

When Walt Jonski's friends did go after Dix two nights later, there were four of them, including Wolf. At his suggestion they left the bikes behind and rode in a dark van with phony plates, a risk Wolf was willing to take. The four, armed only with baseball bats and a tactical knife Wolf carried, wore black clothing, gloves, and black ski masks. They donned their gear inside the van when they parked outside Dix's tract home at one in the morning. Roderick tossed two thick steaks over the backyard's chain-link fence, quickly silencing a pair of dogs.

Roderick crept to the van. "We're in luck. Our boy's zoned out in front of his TV."

"Anyone else?" said Wolf.

He shook his head. "Negative as far as I can tell."

"The dogs good?"

"They said to tell you thank you for the steaks."

"Okay," said Wolf, pulling the ski mask over his face. "Here we go, gentlemen. Stay focused."

They spilled from the van, Wolf leading. He sent Vinny, a Marine recon veteran he had handpicked, to puncture all four tires on a Dodge Charger sitting in the carport. Poised at the front door in a conga line, Roderick led them in, a huge booted foot splintering the cheap front door. Their luck

held. Dix, shirtless and barefooted, was still where Roderick
had seen him—sprawled in front of a large flat-screen TV.
The screen provided ample light to begin their mission.
Despite being drunk, Dix attempted to rise, his feet tangled
in a game controller, crushed beer cans spilling from his lap.

"WHAT THE..."

Wolf leaped at him, delivering a blow to Dix's jaw,
stunning him. The big man dropped to the floor. While
Wolf cleared the other rooms, Roderick and Vinny
immobilized Dix's ankles with duct tape. Duke pulled
the unconscious man's hands above his head, taped
them, and pinned them to the floor with his knees. Wolf
returned and stretched a piece of duct tape across Dix's
mouth. He tugged their prisoner's jeans and underwear
down around his ankles.

"Get some water," he said to Vinny. "Lock the back
door. Draw the blinds. Check on the dogs again. We
don't want any surprises."

"Roger that."

Wolf nodded at Roderick. "Kill the TV."

"Roger that."

Vinny came back with a bowl of water and handed it
to Wolf.

"Dogs?"

"Happy as pigs in shit."

"Perfect. Hold on to him when he comes to." Wolf
tossed the water in Dix's face, then slapped him awake.
He held the spec ops knife's curved blade inches from
Dix's nose when he awoke.

"Okay, asshole, here's the deal. You broke our friend's
leg, didn't you? Keep fucking with our friend and you'll be
singing in a boys' choir."

Wolf waved the knife in front of the bound man's
terrified eyes. He ran the flat of the blade down Dix's

abdomen, and then probed his testicles with the tip of the knife. "I will personally cut your balls off next time. Am I getting through to you?"

A panicked nodding, a muffled voice. Mewing sounds.

"Big brave man. Had to slap a lady around, huh?"

Dix's head dropped back against the carpet with a thud.

"Shit, he fainted. Get more water," Wolf said.

Vinny came back with the bowl and doused Dix, waking him. Wolf probed with the blade again. "You're a real piece of shit, you know that? Consider this your only warning. You so much as come within a mile of our friend and you're done. Nod if you understand me."

A frenzied shaking of the head up and down.

"As a reminder, I'm going to leave you with a memento of our visit. Consider it your only warning." Wolf put away his knife, stood over Dix, bat in hand. "Do not make me come back again."

He brought the bat down on Dix's bare left leg, cracking the tibia mid-point. A muted scream was stifled by the duct tape and Dix fainted again.

"Oh, geez, he pissed himself," said Duke. "Figures."

"We're out of here," ordered Wolf. He severed the duct tape holding Dix's wrists and ankles and pocketed the scraps. He ripped the tape from Dix's mouth and followed the others to the front door.

Gunny Roderick glanced at the deserted street. Nothing moved. No lights in neighboring houses, the only sounds a dog howling in a backyard mid-block and a fading siren.

"Good to go," he whispered.

He gave a wave and the three followed him from the house, Wolf the last man out. They drove away without speaking. The avenging visit had taken twelve anxious minutes from start to finish. Clockwork.

Once on the highway, Duke finally broke the silence. "Like I said, 'Get in, get his attention, deliver the message, get out.'"

"An eye for an eye," said Roderick, "or maybe, a leg for a leg."

Duke patted Wolf's back, said, "Outstanding, Skipper."

Despite their success, Wolf, aware of the risk he had taken, said nothing.

Chapter 37

Sam McFadden awoke to a low rumble coming from his driveway. Shuffling to the window overlooking the front of the house, he raised the blinds to find two bikers dismounting in his driveway. McFadden came back in the bedroom.

"Reggie, why are there Harleys in our driveway?"

He heard a muffled, "Ask Tom...about that."

McFadden stepped into a pair of sweatpants, pulled on a T-shirt, and padded downstairs. Wolf was heading out the side door to the garage with foam cups and a steaming carafe.

"Mind telling me what's going on, Wolfman?"

"Hold that thought, Sam. I just want to bring these guys some coffee."

Bring the guys some coffee? McFadden shook his head and went back upstairs to shower and dress.

Reggie stirred, saying something about temporary security at the house that Wolf had arranged, then fell back asleep. McFadden vaguely recalled a previous conversation along those lines. When he came downstairs to the kitchen, Wolf was nowhere to be seen. McFadden poured himself a mug of coffee and went to the front porch.

I'm not dreaming, there ARE hogs in my driveway.

"Morning, Sam. Let me introduce the guys." A grinning Wolf ushered McFadden to a pair of parked bikes. Wolf said, "Lenny Orton, meet Sam McFadden." A balding barrel-shaped rider stuck out his hand.

Orton had an iron grip. "A pleasure, Sam. Semper Fi."

"And over here...Roderick." McFadden shook the hand of a taller bearded biker. Wolf said, "These Marines are the first of the volunteers pulling security for the next two or three weeks Sam."

On the spot, McFadden lifted his coffee mug. "Appreciate it, gentlemen."

"Our pleasure," they said in unison.

"We blocking your way?" said Orton. "We can move the bikes."

"Nah, you're fine where you are. Thanks, guys."

Wolf hustled McFadden inside and shut the door behind him. "The security detail, remember? We talked about it a couple days ago."

"I admit to not paying close attention when you proposed it. But it's still a shock to wake up to the smell of exhaust and the sound of bikes this early."

"I hear you. Man, those hogs are loud."

Followed by Wolf, McFadden retreated to the kitchen. "You really think we need this?"

Wolf snagged a bagel and took a seat in the breakfast nook. "Absolutely. The price is right—it's free. The guys are happy to do it."

"What did you have to do to arrange this?"

Wolf mumbled, "You don't want to know."

"Was it legal?"

Wolf spread cream cheese on the bagel without answering.

Sighing, McFadden said, "Never mind. Some things are better left unsaid. I'll be hearing from my neighbors before the day is out."

"They don't have some nut job looking for them," growled Wolf despite a mouthful of bagel. "Besides, you heard the cops, Sam. They won't post a stakeout with what little they have to go on at this point."

McFadden sipped his coffee. "You got me there. Even the feds said they couldn't spend resources on investigating something that may not even happen."

"I pray they're right." Wolf finished his bagel. He thumbed over his shoulder at the sidewalk in the backyard. "If it's okay with you, Sam, I'll route these guys to the guesthouse if they need to use the head."

"Do what you need to." He winked at Wolf. "Besides, they look too old to make it past lunch without multiple breaks."

"These guys are not paper tigers, Sam."

"Well, maybe Reggie will feel better having them around. See if you can get them to park their bikes in the garage while I'm gone."

"No can do. We have to make a statement to whoever's out there. We want this guy to see your watchdogs."

"Are they armed?"

Wolf nodded. "I gave them your scatter gun, but don't worry, they won't step off your property."

"You're just full of surprises, aren't you?" McFadden got up from the table.

"Let's hope our mystery man doesn't decide to pay us another visit by coming up the hills behind us like he did before."

"I'll cover that for you until I have to head back to work next week."

Grabbing his laptop case, McFadden said, "If it wasn't so serious this would be amusing. I mean, Harleys in my driveway?"

Wolf began slicing bagels for the toaster.

"You feeding these guys as well?" said McFadden.

"It's a twenty-four-seven deal, Sam. They'll switch off after lunch. I've got pizza and beer lined up for lunch and the night crew."

McFadden sighed. "Pizza. Beer. Bikers. Who knew?"

Wolf was upbeat. "Think of the money we're saving the taxpayers."

"There's your silver lining," said McFadden on his way to the garage. "I'll buy the pizza and beer."

"Knew you would. Semper Fi, Sam."

Chapter 38

Late afternoon, Cesar pulled his van into the carport and carried a six-pack of beer to the kitchen door. He knocked twice. Sparrow peered from behind the blind and lowered his Beretta. He let Cesar in and locked the door behind him.

Cesar giggled. "Hey, *manong*, what's with no more hair?"

"You like it?" Sparrow tucked the pistol at the small of his back. "Tala did it."

"Looking different."

"That's the point."

Tala awoke and wandered to the kitchen. She leaned against the doorframe, heard Sparrow say, "I have a plan, Cesar. I need your help to make this work."

"What you need?"

Sparrow handed him a folded one hundred dollar bill. The thin man snatched the money and pocketed it.

"I need you to get me some old clothes, a long-sleeve shirt and baggy work pants. Also a straw hat and some gardening tools and gloves. You understand what I want?"

"Yeah, I get it. You make like a yard man, eh?"

"One more thing. Tala wants baby powder and a long, dark hooded robe."

"Sure. No problem. Hey, you out of food? I can get more, you know."

"We have enough. But we need the other things. Better you go now, eh?"

"Why the rush?"

Sparrow waved another folded bill. "It's important. You get one more of these when you get back."

"You got it." A smiling Cesar pushed from the chair and eased out the side door to the carport where he had parked his van. Sparrow watched him go.

"You think he'll come back?" she said.

"Of course. His kind thinks only about money."

One hour later, Cesar returned with his purchases and climbed from the van.

Tala took the bags and went to a back bedroom. Cesar grabbed a bottle of beer from the fridge and settled at the small kitchen table opposite Sparrow. He said, "I called Biggie, told him what we doing."

"Why?" bristled Sparrow. "Fool. He had no need to know. Besides, if the police find him they may force him to tell them what he knows about us. Better he didn't know."

Cesar pouted. "He wouldn't like that. You don't know Biggie."

"*Walang problema*—I'll talk to him, make it right."

"He got his own trouble," said Cesar. "I'm the only one running the show for him. Everybody depending on me now. Not easy, *manong*."

Tala came back in the kitchen. She held up an apple and piece of bread.

"We're living like animals," she snapped. "When are we going to leave this hole?"

"*Asong babae*," scolded Cesar. "Biggie doing everything he can. You not the only one, you know."

Venom in her eyes, she glared at him. "Who you calling a bitch? You the one acting like Biggie's bitch." Cesar rose, fists balled, forcing Tala to retreat.

"Sit down," said Sparrow, on his feet, waving the loaded Beretta.

Cesar sat as ordered. "Better talk to her, *manong*." Wary eyes fixed on the pacing Sparrow, he said, "Can't stay long. Biggie depending on me. Better I be going."

Pouring himself a cup of coffee, Sparrow said, "He can wait. Right now what we have to do is more important. We need to talk."

A spark of defiance in Cesar's voice. "Hey, maybe you don't know, but I work for Biggie not you."

"I don't forget," said Sparrow. He stood opposite Cesar, gun in his right hand, coffee in the left. "Change of plans. We're going to need your keys to the van."

"What?"

"The keys. We need your van."

"What? No way, *manong*. Why you want my van? You supposed to stay out of sight till Biggie say the coast is clear."

"That won't work for us," said Sparrow. "We need to move. How can we do that on foot?"

"That's your problem," snarled Cesar. "Call Biggie. He'll say stay put."

Sparrow pressed the Beretta's muzzle against Cesar's forehead. "I'm not asking him, I'm asking you. No, I'm telling you. Give me the keys."

"Fuck you, *manong*."

Frozen in the doorway, Tala listened to yet another bad turn.

Cesar's angry eyes caught hers. "Tala, tell this crazy *pinoy* put down the gun."

"Do what he says, Cesar. Give him the keys."

"You *loko*," he snarled. "Both of you."

Sparrow waved the gun. "The keys."

Cesar made a show of reaching for his jean pocket, stalling for time. "Think about what you doing. Biggie come after you, man."

"Biggie's not coming after anyone," said Sparrow. "He's hiding. The police will find him long before they find us."

"Don't count on it, *manong*." His voice softened. "Hey, no need for the gun. I can help you. We can work together. I can drive you wherever you want."

"Don't trust him," Tala said.

"I don't."

Cesar held up the keys. "Okay, okay, you can have the van."

Sparrow put down the coffee and reached for them. Cesar twisted, reaching for the handgun tucked at the small of his back.

Sparrow swept the cup of steaming coffee at Cesar's face.

Screaming in pain, Cesar shielded his scalded eyes with his left hand, fumbled for his pistol with his right.

Sparrow fired.

Falling backwards, Cesar upended the chair, his right arm pinned beneath him, blood splattering the plaster wall and baseboards. His eyes open, Cesar shuddered once and was still, blood pooling beneath his skull on the yellowed linoleum. Keeping the Beretta pointed at Cesar's head, Sparrow prodded him with a foot. Nothing. Again. Satisfied he was dead, Sparrow snagged the keys and Cesar's cellphone. He grabbed the dead man's pistol and handed it to a stunned Tala.

"We have time. Cut your hair if you wish. Use the powder to make your disguise. I will change clothes and become another faceless gardener."

She fled to the bathroom, Cesar's blood on her shoes and jeans.

His hands under Cesar's arms, Sparrow dragged his body into the living room and propped him in a chair. The dead man's head lolled to one side, his sightless eyes fixed in a stare.

"When you are done pack what you need," he called to Tala. "We have to go."

Shaking, Tala hacked at her hair, then powdered it. She donned the robe over her bloodied jeans and then slipped past Cesar's body without looking. She loaded the van with her belongings, and then went back for food and water, filling a box from the refrigerator. She crawled behind the driver's wheel with the dead man's pistol in her lap.

Sparrow packed his nylon bag and returned to the living room. Kneeling at the curtain's hem, he flicked a lighter. A tiny tongue of flame licked at the fabric and in minutes, the drapes were burning. Sparrow hurried outside, told Tala to start the engine and back down the driveway. She drove away, the rambler's picture window a glowing frame when they reached the corner. By the time they got on the freeway, the home had become Cesar's pyre.

Chapter 39

Looking every bit the anonymous Asian couple, Sparrow and Tala drove east on Mira Mesa Boulevard. In the side mirror, a plume of dark smoke curled in the afternoon sky. The first of the sirens warbled in the distance. They passed under the sluggish interstate and followed the serpentine Scripps Ranch Boulevard up the hill. Nearing the summit, they passed a small park and playground on their right.

"Remember this place," said Sparrow, pointing. "You can wait for me there." Tala glanced at the few cars parked there and returned her eyes to the curving road in front of her. She turned at the top of the ridge—into McFadden's neighborhood overlooking Lake Miramar. Aside from several cars in driveways and a solitary nanny pushing a stroller, the cross street and McFadden's stretch of pavement were deserted.

"There, the house under construction," said Sparrow, indicating the partially completed mansion. "The driveway is long. Park at the end. No one will spot the van from the street." Tala did as told, easing to a stop halfway into the yawning unfinished three-car garage. She killed the engine, certain her beating heart echoed louder than the ticking of the cooling engine.

"Do you remember when we first climbed up there?"

She nodded without speaking.

"It will be different this time," he said. "McFadden will not insult me as he did that day. It amuses me that he doesn't know he owes his life to you."

"Tell me what you are going to do."

"You will leave me here and drive back to the car lot of that small park we passed." He gripped her hand to steady her. "Wait for me there."

"I can do it."

"Of course you can. You are the key to my success, dear Tala."

"What if we have been seen?"

"A small enough risk. No one will notice us here. I am going to find a way into McFadden's house. Then, I wait for him to return home and kill him."

He leaned across the cab and kissed Tala. "You can do your part," he said.

"Don't go," she pleaded. "We still have time."

He caressed her cheek. "I am determined, Tala. When I am finished I will call your cellphone. If all goes well I shall come to you at the park and we will disappear. If you don't hear from me, drive away. You understand?"

She nodded without looking at him.

"I must go before McFadden comes. Leave me." He got out of the van, the pistol tucked beneath his long-sleeved work shirt. Wearing a broad straw laborer's hat as part of his gardener's disguise, he shooed her away. Clippers in hand, he slipped through a side door in the garage shell, heading for the low wall separating the empty mansion's property from McFadden's backyard.

Tala backed slowly from the long driveway and circled the cul-de-sac before heading back down the highway.

Keeping to the lengthening shadows, Sparrow followed the thick hedges along the perimeter of McFadden's patio. Music drifted from the house, a muted light classical tune. Sparrow crept across a narrow path paved with large, square reddish tiles. He followed it to a side door. *Garage*, he thought. Locked. He retraced his steps to the backyard, peered around the corner.

"HEY!"

Sparrow turned to face a large, bearded, shotgun-wielding man blocking the tiled path alongside the house. The garage's access door clicked shut behind the big man.

Not McFadden. Who?

"What the hell you doing?" bellowed the man. "Little late for gardening, don't you think?"

Groping behind his loose shirt for the Beretta, Sparrow bowed slightly, pointing with the clippers in his other hand. "Forgive me, sir. The door was open. I was just leaving."

"Who are you?"

Smiling deferentially, Sparrow risked a step forward. "I am Felix Wong, the McFadden's gardener. I was working in the backyard."

"BULLSHIT!"

"Excuse me, sir?"

"Bullshit! Don't you understand plain English, asshole?"

The bearded man leveled the shotgun, his eyes zeroed in on Sparrow. He took a threatening step forward, raised a cellphone. "Miss Reggie. Got a visitor. Backyard. He..."

Sparrow pulled the Beretta and fired twice, dropping the sentinel.

A woman's panicked voice from the cellphone. "Hello! Hello!"

McFadden's wife? Hopefully, alone.

Sparrow tossed the clippers and raced across the manicured lawn. A pool, its waterfall bubbling at one end, took up most of the yard. A small guesthouse, dark, deserted, overlooked the hillside he and Tala had climbed a lifetime ago. He took brief refuge in an alcove with a stainless steel grill and a glass-topped table set for an evening meal. So close he could feel the closed grill's heat, he thought, *McFadden not home yet. Good.*

The movement of a fleeting shadow in the glass door caught his eye. Gambling, he tried a patio door to the kitchen. It opened, and he slid inside McFadden's house without being challenged. A single set of footsteps pounded the stairs above him. He went from room to room on the first floor. Empty.

Sparrow crossed the front hallway's polished marble floor and unlocked the home's front door. He now had a path of retreat if needed. He cracked open the door, a mistake. A chime rang out, startling him.

A woman's shrill voice above. "Who's there?"

McFadden's wife. Folding himself against a recessed doorway leading to a closet, Sparrow held his breath.

Go upstairs? Make the lady come to me? He hesitated.

Fool! She will be phoning, he thought. *Go up before she calls.*

Sparrow stepped out from his niche. Planting a foot on the stairs, he stared at the muzzle of a .357 Magnum cannon in small hands. She stood just five steps away on carpeted stairs, the black Smith & Wesson revolver centered on his chest.

"Stay where you are!" Reggie McFadden slipped a cellphone from her left pocket. Now one-handed, she ordered, "Do not move. I am calling the police."

"Surely, madam, this a misunderstanding."

"I don't think so. I heard a shot."

He glanced down. His gardener's shirtfront wore traces of blood.

She knows. Now or never.

Sparrow leaped to his right, reaching for his gun. She fired, the hollow point slug shredding his left heel. Screaming to wake the dead, she retreated to the top of the stairs. A thin splatter of blood marked Sparrow's trail across pristine marble.

He limped around the corner, his pistol leading. His wound stung, made him hobble, but didn't disable him. He found his way to the kitchen. To staunch the bleeding he stuffed a towel in his sandal where his heel had been and went looking for her.

A glance at the reflection in a framed glassed print on the wall told him the top of the stairs had been abandoned. He heard a door slam. Sparrow dragged his left foot up the stairs, smearing bright red drops on each tread. Sweeping his weapon back and forth in front of him, he checked three empty bedrooms, a hall bathroom, and an office. No sign of the woman.

At the end of a wide, carpeted hallway, a pair of stout oak doors defied him. Dropping on his belly, Sparrow crawled along one side of the hall, pistol pointed at the twin doors. He fired four shots, then three more at the door's bronzed handles. Wood splintered. Metal sparked, finally giving way. Standing, his back against the wall, Sparrow jammed his gun into his waistband and picked up a wooden bench.

Using it as a shield, he battered the damaged door, attempting to breach it. He got four rapid shots in reply, three chipping the plaster inches from his head. The fourth bullet shattered a picture frame, showering him with glass fragments. His naked scalp bled from needle-like shards.

Crouching, Sparrow hurled the bench against the door in a new attempt. Three more shots drove him to his knees.

An alarm, shrill, jarring, wailed throughout the house. He fired the pistol's remaining rounds, finally separating the door halves. He loaded a second magazine, jacked a round in the chamber, and leaped at the entry, scattering six shots as he bulled his way into the master bedroom. She was gone. He stepped on scattered live rounds spilled from an abandoned box dropped during her flight.

Another barrier. A bathroom door at the end of a walk-in closet, her last refuge. The locked door enraged him. *This she-devil would not die. This woman, McFadden's wife, proving hard to kill. Not supposed to be like this*, he thought.

Sparrow emptied a second magazine through the door and the walls of the bathroom on both sides of the door. *Surely, she could not survive.* The ruined door drifted open, its brass handle dented, hanging useless.

He reloaded and limped forward, using his good foot to prod open the door. He found a broken window, a leaking stool and large pieces of glass shower doors scattered across a marble floor. A mirror above twin sinks was a span of spider webbed glass.

Where did she go? There was no way out.

He heard the distinctive click of a hammer behind him. Turning, his last sight was of her perched on the top of a cabinet in the walk-in closet.

Chapter 40

Detective Mike McManus and two squads, alerted by the dispatcher, had showed not long after the final shots. Wearing a protective vest, he and two uniformed officers cleared each room, beginning on the ground floor. Four cops simultaneously swept the grounds and deserted house next door.

Fearing the worst, McManus and his team took the stairs two steps at a time, tracking the carnage in the silent house. He announced their approach with each step, unsure what they would discover.

McManus found Reggie McFadden frozen in place, her right hand digging into the revolver's black rubber grip, the gun's eight-round cylinder holding empty casings. She had hit Sparrow in the sternum, neck, and chin with sledgehammer hollow-point rounds, each wound fatal. He had fallen back, legs folding under him, mouth open in surprise, the Beretta slipping from his lifeless hand as he toppled.

Following on McManus's heels, McFadden arrived. McManus told the officers blocking the door to let him upstairs. Only when Reggie saw him did she surrender the pistol and allow herself to be helped down from her perch. Once in McFadden's arms, she collapsed. A glance at a sheet hastily torn from the bed and draped over Sparrow's corpse sent renewed shudders through her shoulders as she shuffled through the bedroom. Stumbling down the stairs on McFadden's arm, she fled to a downstairs bathroom and vomited.

Paramedics checked her over as she clung to Sam. Wrapped in a blanket, she accepted a glass of water and sank against a sofa in shock. Her home crawled with crime technicians, police photographers and detectives. A pair of FBI agents arrived. The two spoke first with McManus, and then McFadden out of earshot. Sam came back to the couch to shield Reggie from questioners until she was coherent enough to talk.

Finally, prompted by McManus, Reggie recited every detail of the bloody melee. At one point, she giggled maniacally while replaying the moment she had confronted Sparrow at the foot of her stairs.

"What was I supposed to think?" she said. "A gardener in my foyer? What was this man thinking, that I wouldn't find it strange?" She shook her head.

McFadden mistook her laughter as a good sign. Her laughter died. She wept "Insanity," she mumbled. He diverted her attention when the coroner's team, their preliminary work done, came down the stairs with a sagging body bag.

"You were magnificent," said McFadden, shielding her head against his shoulder. "Your instincts were spot on. You did what you had to do."

"Damn fine marksmanship," added McManus.

"Sam's training," she wailed through tears.

"Hate to see it end up like this," he said. "Better him than you on the floor upstairs. I don't want to think about how this might have turned out differently."

"Is that who you and Detective McManus think it is?" she said.

"Sparrow? It fits. We'll know more when they finish their investigation."

"I can't stay here, Sam."

"I know, I know." He didn't press. "We'll get you up to your mother's. I've already called her to let her know what happened."

"Roderick's dead, isn't he?"

"Yeah. Sorry, Reggie. They took him away a few minutes ago. McManus says it appears he must have confronted this guy early on, based on your statement and the position of his body."

"He called me, Sam. Warned me we had an intruder. I heard a shot."

"I know. That's what he was there for."

"He saved my life. Gave me time to run upstairs." She cried. "He's a hero."

"I'll let his guys know. We owe him. Owe them all. I'm glad Wolfman talked me into having those Marines around. Hate to think what would have happened if he hadn't been here."

She nodded, dabbing her eyes with a tissue. "I think the killer was after you, Sam. He would have been here, waiting for you to come home if Roderick hadn't stopped him."

"You're the one who stopped him, sweetheart." McFadden pulled Reggie to her feet. "You probably saved my life. Look, I'm going to tell McManus I'm taking you to Santa Barbara to your mother's. Give me a minute."

She clung to him. "Don't leave me alone, Sam."

He kissed her forehead and pulled her tight against him, a private moment despite the small army of police securing the crime scene that had been their home.

Wolf arrived, berating himself for his absence.

"I was on a run with the guys, Sam. Sorry."

"Forget it. Reggie's safe. That's all that matters."

He got a briefing from McManus, talked to McFadden, and hugged a tearful Reggie. Uncharacteristically quiet, he stood off by himself, surveying the scene.

McFadden said to him, "Got to get Reggie out of here Wolfman. It's a circus."

"Roger that, Sam. You going up to Santa Barbara?"

"Yeah, best place for her right now."

"Want me to tag along as security?"

McFadden put a hand on Wolf's shoulder. "Thanks, but no need. Keep an eye on this place for me until I get back. And keep the shop open. I'll call the guys."

"Will do. I've got my gear in the guesthouse anyway. I'll stay around."

"Appreciate it."

After a final check with the EMTs and another short chat with McManus, Reggie and McFadden waited for the chaos to settle. They secluded themselves in his den to avoid an impromptu press conference in the driveway with a deputy chief. The briefing ended with shouted questions and generic answers.

Summoned to finish it, McManus stepped forward. "That's it, folks. We'll have a more complete statement tomorrow. You'll get everything we know. Thank you."

Two TV satellite vans parked mid-block finished "live" shots with their reporters, broke down their gear, and left. A news helicopter dipped in a final pass and soared away. Eventually, small knots of neighbors on the fringe of the day's madness drifted home, their heads nodding with gossip.

The police cleared out. One squad car stayed behind to cordon off the perimeter with the familiar yellow tape, securing the scene from the curious. With McManus's okay, Wolf reclaimed his spot in the pool guesthouse with a promise to stay out of the main house, a crime scene. He called Crystal Hamm and told her what he knew. He had a sleepless night ahead of him.

Crime scene tape circled hedges and tree trunks, fluttering in the evening breeze. Shielded by McManus and a uniformed officer, Reggie and McFadden finally got in Sam's car and backed from the driveway. Anonymous in the traffic, they drove down the hill in the gathering dark, passing a nearby roadside playground and its empty lot without looking back.

Chapter 41

Biggie Pacheco's balding porcine lawyer had twice given his opinion and was soundly rejected. He tried one last time. "Let me arrange your surrender to the police. We'll go in together." Met with silence, he threw up his hands and packed his briefcase.

"Turn yourself in," he said. "The longer you're out, the worse it looks."

Biggie, wearing his usual mesh T-shirt, shorts and sandals, sank back against a sagging couch in his one remaining safe house. "Not ready."

"The police are in no mood to negotiate. The next knock on your door will be the SWAT team. I'm your best hope right now and I'm telling you to give it up."

"I'll call you," said Pacheco, unmoved.

The lawyer got to his feet and shoved a briefcase under his arm. "You know my number." He headed for the barricaded steel door where one of Biggie's few remaining loyalists stood guard. The nameless sentinel undid four heavy deadbolts and stepped outside to make sure it was safe. He ducked back inside and nodded. Pacheco's lawyer slipped away in the night. The locks were set and the guard dog was sent upstairs to take his place at a narrow window overlooking the street.

"Two hundred dollars an hour for five-dollar advice," grumbled Biggie.

He heaved himself from the couch and went to a back bedroom. He rapped twice and entered. A battered brass table lamp on an end table cast a weak yellow half-moon across the sparsely furnished room. Tala, still wearing her dark hooded robe, lounged on a ragged love seat, a bottle of water in hand. A frowning Filipina wearing skintight leathers and spikey bleached androgynous cut, leaned against the wall, tattooed arms folded, a butterfly knife in one hand. Biggie straddled a chair, said, "Leave us, Rita."

Pushing from her corner, the woman sauntered past Pacheco, twirling her knife, and left the two alone.

"Cy says to turn myself in," he said. "What you think, Tala?"

"Maybe you should listen to him. They looking for you, you know."

"Looking for you, too, Tala."

She scowled. "That why you have your bitch watching me? Afraid I'll run?"

"Where you gonna run to? You wanna take Cy's advice, turn yourself in?"

"I should have stayed with Sparrow," she said, avoiding the question and Biggie's eyes. "I could have helped him."

Biggie got up and paced the small room, hands laced behind his head, his eyes on the ceiling's peeling plaster. "Good thing you wasn't there. McFadden's woman was tough, man. No place for you to be when it went down. Sparrow knew that. That's why he went alone."

"We didn't expect to find a bodyguard."

"McFadden no fool, Tala. Those people had to know you were coming."

"What if I went away for a while?"

"Where? Mexico? You wouldn't last a week, girl. The feds involved now. Think about it, Tala. They got your face. Your name."

"What do you think I should do?"

Returning to the chair planted in front of the small couch, Biggie sat down, his eyes locked with Tala's. "The way I see it you only got two choices." He paused, waiting for her to take his bait.

"What choices?"

"One, you go to the cops. I can fix it with Cy. He takes you in, stands up for you in court. Maybe you do okay with his help."

"I'd do time, Biggie. You know that."

He shrugged. "You right. You would do some time most likely."

Tala got up, walked to the curtained window, peeked out, and returned to her seat. "I wouldn't last inside. You know that. Too many enemies."

"Right again. You nevah should have rolled over for Sparrow, girl."

Tala threw him a resentful look. "Not your business, Biggie."

"Yeah, it was. You don't see how that whole thing turned our place inside out. Take Manny. Fool loved you, Tala. You walked on water for that boy."

She stared at the floor. "I never encouraged him."

"Didn't have to. That day we picked up Sparrow from the airport I knew things was going to get bad. When he beat your ass in *eskrima* I knew he was going to be a problem for you."

"He was good."

"Too good."

"You made some money on the match betting against me."

"Hey, so I get lucky for once. Fringe benefit. But it kinda threw things outa balance, you know?"

"We were obligated to give him shelter. You said so yourself."

"We had no choice, you see? The Manila bosses set this up. Had to cooperate. I nevah thought it would be for this long. Once I figured out what he was here to do I knew it was going to be a disaster, you know?"

"You said I had two choices. What's the second one?"

"Revenge. Go after McFadden. Finish it. That would put us in the clear with our people in Manila."

"If Sparrow couldn't do it what makes you think I could?"

Biggie leaned forward, his hand tapping Tala's knee. "Don't have to kill the man himself."

Confused, Tala said, "I thought you said..."

"You only have to make sure it happens."

"How is this possible?"

He waved away her hesitation. "That is not the question to ask. The question is—Would you do it if you could?"

Tala stiffened. "Of course. McFadden deserves to die, same for his wife."

"I agree. Though his wife is of no concern."

"She killed Sparrow, Biggie."

"Tala, think on this. If McFadden is killed, I think his wife is as good as dead. It's McFadden our people in Manila after. They have their own agenda and we have ours. You can finish McFadden if you willing."

"I'm willing."

"Good. I want you to meet someone, Tala. A person who can accomplish this. A man well suited to do what Sparrow could not do."

"One of ours?"

"Much better. One of theirs."

"Theirs? I don't understand."

Biggie rose, offering his hand. "Come. I introduce you."

Chapter 42

Tala got to her feet and followed Biggie down a corridor to a dimly lit back room at the rear of the house. He knocked on a closed door and entered.

Sitting cross-legged on a thin mattress on the floor, a wiry Filipino cleaning a stripped handgun glanced up as the two entered. His deep-set eyes, yellow with jaundice, burned with intensity beneath shaggy brows in a furrowed face.

His was a monastic room. Aside from the bed, a small stationary fan and lamp were the only furnishings. An open suitcase of clothing lay on the hardwood floor.

Biggie said, "Hey, *manong*, this is..."

"Tala. Yes, I know." Setting aside a linen cloth lined with the gun's oiled parts, the stranger got to his feet and circled her. "Biggie tell me about you. How things did not go as planned. How you were deceived. Is not your fault."

Unnerved by the man's menacing stare and presumption, Tala retreated, her back to the wall. "What you mean, deceived?"

The stranger shot a quizzical look at Biggie. "You tell her nothing, *kuya*?"

"Not yet, *manong*."

The stranger stepped back. "Tell her what happened."

Tala said, "What's he mean, Biggie?"

"The man we knew as Sparrow was not who we thought he was."

The stranger interrupted in tagalog. "*Isang huwad.*"

Tala shook her head. "An imposter?"

"Yes, yes. Correct." Pleased at being understood, the man said, "My English is okay, not the best. But you were lied to by this person. Not your fault."

"What lies?" Tala braced her palms against the wall. "That can't be true. We knew him as Sparrow. He was sent here. You expect us to believe you? To trust you?"

"Of course. I arrive only yesterday. I am under orders."

"We got a call. I had to send Rita to pick him up," Biggie said. "I haven't been on the streets since the cops raided our old place."

Biggie turned to her. "We accepted Sparrow in good faith but he lied."

"What are you talking about?"

"We got taken, Tala. Your boy was not the real deal."

"Our friend here tells me the man we welcomed actually worked for him as a stand-in. A decoy. No one knew, you understand?"

"No, I don't. Why would he risk his life for a lie? This doesn't make sense. Explain, Biggie."

"The one staying with us, the one who called himself Sparrow, took a large amount of money from a man who hired him to arrange a hit on McFadden."

"Yes, it was not his to keep," said Biggie's guest. "The name or the money. Both belong to me."

Bewildered, Tala slid down the wall, hugging her knees, grappling with what she was hearing. Biggie squatted in the corner, opposite the mattress on which the newcomer had resumed his cross-legged pose. A study in tranquility, the man began assembling the pistol. Flashing a reptilian grin, a single incisor, gold in the low light. He said, "Not to worry, Lady Tala. It does not matter now who hired me to kill this McFadden. The man who sent me does not need to know what happened here. I will right things and return to collect what is rightfully due me. You will see."

"This is crazy," she said. "I'm supposed to just accept this, all that's happened and I'm...we're supposed to trust a complete stranger?"

"We have to," said Biggie.

"It's not that simple," she said.

Biggie thought differently. "Why not? He wants McFadden dead. His people want McFadden dead. You and I want McFadden dead. He can do this."

"Yes, *walang problema*—no problem. I finish this and return to Manila."

"And he wants us to help him?" she said to Biggie.

"Yes. That's where you come in. Show him where McFadden lives. He will take it from there. Let him do it, Tala. He takes the risk, not you."

"And what about me?"

"What about you? Do what he asks. Then we find you a safe place."

"And if I refuse?"

Biggie's voice flattened. "Answer to Manila or take your chances with the cops."

"I need to think about this."

"No you don't. Just do what he asks. End of story. Stay here tonight."

"Then what?"

Biggie got to his feet. "Then you help him. We have to move fast before the cops put it together and come for us."

"I want to be by myself...to think."

Biggie rose. "Not a problem. Stay in your room. Nobody mess with you."

"I don't want Rita anywhere near me."

"Okay."

Biggie and Tala left the new arrival to himself. Biggie walked Tala to her room and gave word to his crew to stay alert. "No one gets in," he said, "no one leaves." He knew Tala's thinking...*Fight or flight. Surrender or flee.* She had few options.

In the morning, Tala gave in to Biggie's demands. She answered every question the Manila assassin asked about

McFadden. Starting with surveillance of his hilltop neighborhood, she told of the aborted climb, and the daring visit to his gun range. She ended with what little she knew of the bloody debacle inside the house. Absorbing each word, the killer methodically went over every detail. Ordered by Biggie to make a food run, a sullen Rita returned and left it on the table without acknowledging Tala or the visitor.

Beyond the walls of the safe house the hunt for Biggie and Tala continued. Biggie's lawyer risked a discreet call to describe the mounting pressure on San Diego streets.

"First, don't tell me anything I shouldn't know," he cautioned. "Consider this a courtesy call, Biggie. You should know there is an ongoing discussion among your peers about how much longer they're willing to put up with the heat they're feeling."

"Ah, chill, Cy. You panic over nothing. It will blow over. It always does."

"Really? Yesterday they picked up Benny and six of his boys. Sweated them for hours before my partner could get them released. And they trashed Avado's clubhouse looking for dope. Anyone the cops find on a corner these days gets a ride downtown."

"Been there myself for all these guys. They know the routine."

"Get my drift, Biggie? Put yourself in their position. Think about it. Give up Tala. She's not worth it. You're gonna end up looking bad. You look bad, I look bad. I have my limits, too, you know. I have to make a living in this town."

"A couple days, Cy," answered Biggie. "That's what I'm thinking."

"That's a lifetime out on the streets, friend."

"I understand."

"I don't think you do. If you really appreciated the seriousness of whatever it is you're doing, you'd come in from the cold. This is my last call."

"I understand. I call you next time."

"I hope you'll still be able to hold a phone. Goodbye."

That afternoon Tala resigned herself to the attempt on McFadden. She tutored the assassin on a laptop, showing him satellite maps of the roads and hills surrounding McFadden's home. A quick study, he traced a route similar to the one she and Sparrow had taken that day by the lake. Drilled in the details of what the killer was planning, she agreed to play what she determined would be a minor part. Biggie, told nothing about what his guest was determined to do, sent Rita shopping for certain supplies the Manila hitman wanted. When she returned in a van, packed with things on the list, the clock began ticking.

Chapter 43

McFadden took the call on his cellphone as he picked his way past a carpet layer working his way up the stairs to the master bedroom. McManus had an update about the case. "We're dead in the water right now, Sam. No sign of Biggie Pacheco or this Tala."

"Not comforting. Did you see the latest update on the news about the shooting this morning?"

"Yeah. A bit over the top for old news. This whole week has been a station manager's wet dream for ratings month."

McFadden said, "No way to keep Reggie out of this, I guess. She saw it on the Santa Barbara station. I've got her stashed at her mother's for a second week."

"Security?" said McManus.

"Her sister's husband is filling in for now."

"My captain says he'll have a unit make the rounds in your neighborhood occasionally. Santa Barbara told us they're keeping an eye out as well."

"My tax dollars at work, huh? Good use as far as I'm concerned."

"Once we take Biggie and Tala off the streets you should be okay."

"Suppose so. I'm waiting for Wolf. He and I are going to Roderick's wake tonight."

"Sad occasion. I'll see you there, Sam. We'll have the funeral home covered."

"That helps. I've got one of the range guys coming to watch the house while we're there."

"Smart. We'll keep looking for these dirt bags."

McFadden said, "Right. Thanks for the call." He pocketed the phone.

From the top of the landing he spotted Wolf parking next to a flooring store's van in the driveway. Wolf followed a tile gofer through the front door and waved to McFadden. He wandered upstairs past the carpet installer and found Sam comparing the merits of beige versus off-white with his painting contractor.

"Hey, Sam. Things are looking good. What a difference a week makes."

"Wolfman, what's your opinion on these colors?" McFadden pointed to four sample squares of paint on the wall where the landing met the stairs.

"Not good with colors, Sam. Reggie's your expert."

"Still in Santa Barbara. Won't be back for another week."

The painting contractor, a patient Hispanic with roller in hand, was begging for a decision. The upstairs sitting room at the top of the stairs, primed and patched six days after the shooting, was a blank canvas. "Which one, señor?"

McFadden looked at Wolf, who said, "I'm not getting involved. I do know there's a law of nature that says if a husband picks a color it will inevitably be the wrong one."

McFadden frowned, turned to the painter and said, "Go with the off-white."

"Which off-white, señor?"

"Hell, I don't know. That one," he said, pointing to the middle swatch. Unruffled, the contractor nodded and opened a can.

Wolf said. "A man of decision, Sam. I like that. Can't get in too much trouble with off-white. You'll still be wrong, of course."

"Well, Reggie can change it when she gets back home," groused McFadden.

"How's she doing?"

"Let's talk outside."

McFadden led the way to the shaded balcony off the sitting room. The spot overlooked the pool. He took a padded rattan chair. Wolf leaned against the wrought iron railing, his back to the pool.

"Gonna be tough the first few days when she gets back," said Wolf.

"I know. She's actually surprised me. Doing much better than I could have hoped for. Being with her mom and sister helped. She's tougher than I thought."

"I coulda told you that." Wolf shook his head. "Close call, Sam. Damn lucky. Shame about Roderick, though. That's eating me up. Seeing his family tonight is gonna be tough."

"That's the worst part about this whole thing."

"I feel it, too, Sam. I'm the one who asked those guys to pull guard duty."

"A lifesaver for Reggie, Wolfman. I owe you...and those guys."

"Maybe some day we can...I dunno, do something for them."

McFadden got up, joined Wolf at the railing. "Absolutely. You come up with an idea and we'll make it happen."

Their conversation was interrupted by a tapping on glass. The painter stood behind the French doors, motioning to the wall with the roller. Wolf laughed. McFadden went inside, inspected the progress and gave a thumbs-up. He took Wolf on a tour of the repaired closet doors and the finishing touches tile installers were doing throughout the bathroom.

"Doing a great job, Tony," said McFadden.

The bearded shop owner was spreading fresh grout across the tiles. "Thanks, Sam. We'll have this looking as good as new. Just like before. You know, before the...ah, sorry." Embarrassed, the craftsman focused on his task.

"I know. It'll be perfect."

McFadden and Wolf went downstairs. "Tony heard about what happened. He came out of retirement just to do the tiling. Reggie always liked his work."

The two snagged cold drinks in the kitchen and went out by the pool. They stood, sipping icy beer in the sun while surveying the lake below, beyond that, San Diego's skyline.

"Seems like all this happened years ago," said Wolf.

Motioning with his beer bottle, McFadden studied the parched hillside. "Remember that day when you called me from down there?"

"Yeah," sighed Wolf. "Who knew?"

"You sensed something, Wolfman. You knew something wasn't right."

"Hindsight, Sam."

"That's what I like about hindsight, it's twenty-twenty."

Wolf said, "Never that simple though, is it?"

"Not ever."

"I got your back, Sam."

"Never doubted it."

Chapter 44

Biggie put his plan in motion. He called his lawyer and announced he was ready to surrender to the cops. The timing, Biggie insisted, would be his call.

Cyrus Hernandez was puzzled. "What? You got somewhere else to be before ten o'clock? What's the big deal, Biggie? Your ride gonna turn into a pumpkin?"

"Make the deal, Cy. I don't care what you tell 'em, just make sure they know we're coming in at ten."

"You make my life hard sometimes, you know that? Maybe I got somewhere I want to be at that time. You ever think about that?"

"Nevah crossed my mind. Ten o'clock, Cy."

"I'll pick you up at twenty till. Don't screw this up, Biggie."

"I'm good. See you then."

"Don't go anywhere. Stay put. Don't forget, your name ain't worth shit on the streets these days."

"I'll be waiting." Biggie shut down his phone and told Rita to follow him to the attached garage. He checked the van. It was loaded with everything the Manila hit man had asked for.

"You going with them tonight, Rita," he said.

A snarl. "Why I gotta go?"

"Because I say so. You think I want Tala out there with our man by herself?"

"You don't trust her, eh?"

"That's right. I want you there."

"Why don't you go yourself then?"

"I gotta be somewhere with Cy." Biggie loomed over her. "You listening to me? What did I just say?"

"You want me to watch her."

"That's right. Very important. You got to make sure she holds up her part of this, you know? Don't want no last minute changes. We gotta make sure our boy from Manila does his job. No turning back, Rita. You got it?"

"Yeah, I got it. That's all you want me to do?"

Holding her chin in his hand, Biggie paused. "Yeah, there's one other thing."

Pulling her close, he whispered in her ear, prompting a cruel smile. Then, he kissed her hard, laughing as she fought him. He released her. Wiping her mouth with the back of her hand, she spit on the floor, and flashed a blade at her side, venom in her voice.

"You ever do that again and I'll..."

"You'll do what?" Biggie, his brow furrowed, said, "You don't know what you missing, Rita." He headed back to the house, saying over his shoulder, "Don't forget. It's on you tonight."

She put away the blade, gagging at the taste of him still in her mouth.

Chapter 45

That night, under a sliver of midnight moon, Tala drove the Manila assassin to Lake Miramar's deserted park. Rita rode in the back of the van, her eyes on the two in the front seat.

Gripping the wheel, Tala said, "You do know the park is closed."

"Not to us," he said, his face grim. "Remember what I tell you?"

"Yes. I just thought..."

"Do what I say."

To avoid being seen entering the closed park, Tala drove another quarter mile on Scripps Lake Drive until they were momentarily alone on the road. At his command, she made a sudden U-turn, returning to the park's entry.

She killed the lights and nosed the van to the locked gates
of steel pipe. A pair of west-bound cars passed on Scripps
Lake Road, their drivers oblivious to the parked van in the
shadows. He got out, the bolt cutter in his hands.

The jaws of the tool bit through the lock and he pushed
open the gates. "For us the park is open," he said, grinning.
"Pull ahead and wait for me."

After closing the gates behind him, he climbed back
in the passenger's seat and told her to follow the
serpentine road up the hill. At the east end of the park's
lot he ordered her to drive a short distance on the paved
trail and stop. Turning in his seat, he handed a small
flashlight to Rita and said, "Get out."

"What? Why? Biggie said nothing about this."

"Not to worry. I want you to walk ahead of us with the
flashlight pointed at the ground to guide us. Keep your
hand tight around the light. Show just enough for Tala to
follow. Stay in the middle of the road."

"I don't know this road. Never been here."

"*Walang problema*," he hissed. "We drive slow behind
you until we reach a safe place to turn around."

"And then?"

"Then, we will return to the spot where Tala climbed
that day."

Rita got out. She came around to the driver's side, her face
inches from Tala's. "Don't think to try anything stupid."

Tala stared ahead without acknowledging the threat.

"Now go," he said, waving his handgun.

Focusing a half-dollar sized circle of light on the pavement,
Biggie's mole stepped off, timidly at first, the flashlight at her
right side. She heard the van slip into gear behind her, the
tires crunching loose gravel.

Tala kept the van centered on the maintenance road
circling the lake. Gaining confidence, Rita increased her

pace, eager to be done with it. The flashlight bobbed against her leg. In fifteen minutes, they reached a cul-de-sac where the pavement ended, the terminus marked by yellow steel posts sunk in the ground. "Only foot traffic and bicycles from this point on," said Tala.

Rita came back to the van. "Why you stopping?"

"This is where we turn around," said Tala. "I will use parking lights on my return."

"Won't we be seen?" she said.

"I don't think so."

Rita climbed back in the van. Tala drove slowly, the pavement familiar on the return trip. She passed a second inlet and stopped, letting the engine idle. "This is where we climbed that day," she said. The three of them got out. He stood between the two women in the dark.

"There." Tala pointed to the ridge above where a few lighted houses sat like beacons.

He turned to Rita, then Tala. "You drive to the street where McFadden lives. Park on the cross street and wait there. I kill McFadden and come to you."

Jacking a round in the Beretta's chamber, he attached a suppressor to the muzzle. "Unload my things," he ordered.

The two women returned to the van and opened the side door. Rita muscled a plastic pump bottle and can of gasoline from the cargo space. Tala followed with a box of flares.

Rita's smiled approvingly. "Ah, of course. Now I understand."

He took the box of emergency flares and flashed a rare smile. "Yes. I come for McFadden behind a wall of fire."

Chapter 46

The Manila assassin worked quickly, carrying the flares and gas-filled pump bottle to the side of the road where the hills rose. Ordering the women back in the van, Tala at the wheel, Rita next to her in the passenger's seat, he leaned in the driver's window. "Stay in the car lot until you first see flames. Then go. Do not hesitate."

"Remember. I will be at the end of the street where he lives. When we next meet, the hills will be on fire and McFadden will be dead."

He slipped around to the passenger window.

"Won't there be confusion with the fire?" said Rita.

"Of course, he said. "I depend on it." He whispered, "You know what you are to do?"

She nodded, her face grim.

He came back to the driver's side. "Go, Tala."

She eased from the spot, rolling forward at a tentative pace until she turned on the parking lights. He watched her disappear around the inlet's curving road, then reappear on the next turn. He got to work.

High above him, McFadden's house was dark save for soft bluish yard lights marking the fenced perimeter. The vacant house next door loomed like an abandoned castle. Across the lake, Tala reached the lot. He saw the van's parking lights wink off.

Good, he thought. *Now, my part.*

He pushed down on the pump's handle until the pressure built. Gripping the bottle, Sparrow began soaking bone-dry brush along the road with a mist of gasoline. He pumped again, spraying bushes along the rocky trail, covering as much of the tinder as he could before the pressure ceased. When the pump was empty, he tossed it aside and reached for the first of his flares. Rubbing the striker against the flare's tip produced a thick finger of angry red fire. He rolled it into the base of a large bush.

WHOOSH.

An explosion of flames. Igniting two more flares, he arced both high overhead at the hillside, one left, one right. Immediately, more tongues of fire, then a dancing line of flames raced across the base of the brush-covered hill. A wall of flame rose, head-high, devouring everything in its path. The winds, fed by the heat, picked up, sending fire toward the distant ridge. Nearly invisible in his black clothes, he tied a bandana over his nose and mouth and began following a beaten path behind the flames, thick smoke covering his ascent.

Chapter 47

Just after midnight, and in the dark, Wolf swam six underwater laps. He surfaced in the deep end and filled his lungs with cool night air. In the distance, San Diego's softened lights glowed through a layer of fog. Wolf lay back, drifting to the shallow end until his feet touched bottom. He climbed out, wrapped himself in a thick towel and wandered to the edge of the patio where it gave way to a fringe of lawn, railings, and plantings. Below was a dark void, beyond that, Lake Miramar and the city.

Wolf's eyes shifted to flickering light reflected in the lake far below. Two thin lines of sparks caught his eyes. As he watched, sparks turned into flame. A ragged line of fire erupted in hills carpeted with tinder—a Californian cliff dweller's worst nightmare.

Wolf took one look and began pounding on the patio doors of the main house bellowing as he did. "FIRE! Sam! Wake up! The hill's on fire!"

Lights came on inside the house. McFadden, barefooted and wearing jeans, threw open the patio doors. "What's going on?"

"The hills," yelled Wolf.

The two ran to where the pool deck ended and the hillside began. Fire stretched across three hills well below the ridgeline. Boiling smoke curled in the night sky, the ugly billows reflecting yellowish light from the crackling inferno.

McFadden, ran inside, came back with his cell, staring at the advancing flames as he spoke. "Fire. Just started minutes ago. North side of the lake. Moving slow but it's going to pick up speed in minutes."

Wolf had retreated to his guest quarters to dress. He came back to the south side of the house where Sam stood, cellphone in hand, feeding information to the dispatcher.

"Trouble," McFadden said, "this entire ridge is in its path if the wind holds."

Wolf stared into the blazing hills below. "We'd better get the cars ready to evacuate if we have to."

Eyes on the flames, McFadden said, "Roger that."

Wolf headed to the garage. Sam yelled after him. "Stage the SUV at the end of the driveway. Grab what's important to you. I'll do the same. And toss some water and clothes in a bag in case we have to get the hell out of here."

Both men threw together what they needed and met again at the edge of the patio. Shaking his head, McFadden said, "No rain for months, years. This place is going to light up like a Roman candle.'

"What's the word from the fire department?" said Wolf.

"On their way. They're fielding a lot of calls."

Wolf put a hand on McFadden's shoulder. "If you're staying, so am I."

McFadden slapped Wolf on the back and showed him a key on a lanyard. "Okay. Pump in the storage locker next to the guesthouse. We can use the pool as backup. Give me a hand. We'll set up between your quarters and the house."

"I'm on it." He followed McFadden. The pair returned with a wheeled pump.

McFadden shut off the filter. "Wolfman, fire hose," he shouted. "In the shed. We need that."

Wolf went back to wrestle one hundred feet of coiled hose across the patio to where McFadden was fueling the pump motor.

"Got a lot of water on hand, Wolfman. We can save this place. Not going without a fight."

Unwinding the hose, Wolf nodded. "You got that right. But you know this is crazy, Sam."

"Yeah, it is. But I'm not losing my home, dammit."

Wolf raised a ladder to the tiled roof. Sirens wailed on the streets below.

Chapter 48

From her perch in the driver's seat, Tala's eyes caught the first spark of fire across the lake. Dousing her lights, she eased the van toward the park's exit road and stopped at the far end of the lot. In the passenger seat, a mesmerized Rita watched a line of flames blossom on the hill as she slipped the knife from her belt. Folding the handle, she readied the blade. Turning from the spectacle in the hills, she yelled.

"What are you waiting for? Go!"

Gripping the wheel, Tala said, "Not yet. The fire has to be higher up the hills."

She felt a hammer blow on her right side and looked down. A blade.

Another blow, higher up, glancing off a rib.

Out of breath, she let go of the wheel, reaching beneath her robe for Cesar's pistol. Offering up her right arm, she fended off a third blow. Rita was on her, snarling, stabbing, thrusting as if possessed.

Tala fired. Rita fell back, dropping the glistening blade. Tala fired again.

She dropped the pistol. Her breathing coming harder. Pressing her right hand against her side, she came away with a palm slick with blood. *That bitch. Biggie.*

Her one thought was to breach the gate and get help. Weaving down the winding road she accelerated, aiming for the center of the exit, her left hand like iron on the wheel.

Halfway down she lost her nerve and hit the brakes, skidding sideways against the concrete divider. Her vision blurred. Backing up, she lined up again for the gate.

She told herself. *Hit hard enough and I'm through. What if someone notices the open gate? So what? I will be long gone.*

One minute passed. She felt her life ebbing away. Tala steeled herself, made the sign of the cross, braced against the seat, and roared down the road. She hit the entrance gate with punishing force, sending the pipes flying open. The impact shattered the left headlight and crushed the van's grill.

Exhilarated, she shrieked in release. Oblivious to a pulsing halo of strobe lights and a bellowing klaxon on her left, she fought the wheel to the right—into the oncoming path of a fully loaded 35,000-pound pumper truck.

Bathed in headlights, Tala opened her mouth to scream.

Chapter 49

Smoke, heavy, acrid, crept toward the ridgeline. A trickle of neighbors' cars filled the streets, jockeying bumper-to-bumper to escape the threat. Heat spun off whirlwinds of sparks that jumped ahead of the creeping wall of flame, seeding new fire in untouched spots.

At McFadden's direction, Wolf dragged a section of canvas hose to the pool's deep end and fed it to the bottom. He handed the other end to Sam at the pump. "How much time we have before it hits the house?" he asked.

"Judging from the wind, ten minutes. If we're lucky, fifteen."

A pair of fire trucks and a pumper, horns blaring, turned off the main road, making little headway upstream against a growing, chaotic line of fleeing cars. Finally, the rigs rumbled over the curb, the drivers taking to the narrow sidewalk, gouging landscaping as they went. Two police squad cars arrived and parked in the median. Four officers got out and started unraveling the knot of panicked drivers. The first wave of ash and embers, borne aloft by the growing heat, drifted over the ridge, dropping on roofs, dusting threatened hedges.

A handful of brave souls, McFadden among them, began spraying water to lessen the threat to their homes. While the amateurs did their best, pandemonium reigned until the professionals got things in hand.

Sweeping the nozzle back and forth, McFadden soaked his roof, the trees, and the most vulnerable sides of his house. Wolf wielded a long-handled shovel, crushing embers falling between McFadden's home and his neighbor's vacated house. Wolf raced to the front yard to snuff sparks. That crisis past, he began filling pails of water from the pool. He was everywhere, dousing one threat after another.

In the abyss below fire ate everything in its path, ravenous for more.

The winds shifted, sending the growing wall of flames marching at the scaffolding rigged around the house next door to McFadden's. Before the flames threatened, intense heat arrived, melting plastic sheeting draping the house. Dangling scraps of plastic danced like strips of charred flesh, turning the air toxic in the inferno. Wolf filled two plastic pails and raced through a curtain of falling water to an exposed part of McFadden's garage where embers drifted. Tossing one bucket at nibbling tongues of flame, Wolf bent to grab the second one. The window above him exploded in a shower of fragments.

Hotter than I imagined, he thought. *Got to get Sam to bring the hose around to this side.*

Wolf reached for the filled bucket. The window frame next to his head splintered, piercing his scalp with slivers of wood. Despite the fire's roar he heard what sounded like a muffled gunshot. A third shot hit the wall, inches from Wolf's face, showering him with stucco fragments. He instinctively dove to the ground.

He's here!

Chapter 50

Wolf wormed his way backwards to the corner of the garage and rose on one knee. A crouching silhouette, framed in the vacant window of the deserted house, crossed his vision. The shadow fired another shot and was just as quickly gone.

Got to warn Sam.

Wolf crabbed around the parked SUV and ran for the pool. "Sam!" he shouted.

"Up here," yelled McFadden from his perch. Pulsing hose draped over his right shoulder, he had climbed a ladder to focus the spray on the roof's south side. Reaching the foot of the ladder braced on patio stones, Wolf scrambled up, yelling at McFadden.

"Sonofabitch, Sam! Another shooter's out there!"

McFadden, beating back the threat from next door, did not respond.

Wolf tugged on the snaking hose. McFadden looked back, puzzled at the interference. Wolf bellowed the word. "SHOOTER," Pointing at the blazing hill, he tried again. "Shooter!"

McFadden didn't get it. Waving Wolf away, he yanked the length of hose from his friend's hands and crawled to the roof's peak wreathed in smoke. About to stand, he clutched his left shoulder in surprise and fell back, dropping the hose. Out of control, the nozzle whipped about, just missing McFadden's head. It slithered back and forth across the red tiles like a crazed serpent. Wolf lunged for it, lost his chance, and watched the hose arch into the pool—of no use at the moment.

In obvious pain, McFadden slid headfirst down the tiles, reaching for Wolf's outstretched hand, but missing. Catching himself at the edge with his right hand, he dangled for one second, and then dropped to the ground, his fall broken by thick hedges. Wolf slid down the ladder and rushed to McFadden. Blood soaked Sam's left shoulder. Dazed, McFadden said, "What happened?"

"Damn nozzle had a mind of its own," lied Wolf. Stripping off his shirt, he folded the fabric and pressed it hard against McFadden's wound. "Keep the pressure on your shoulder. Stay put. I'll find some EMT guys."

McFadden tried to rise. "Wolfman, the fire hose."

"Don't worry. It's not going anywhere." He squeezed McFadden's hand, then headed for one of the parked fire rigs.

Wolf returned with two fire department medics and a pair of cops, one a sergeant he had met following the shootout at McFadden's house. Wolf stood back as the EMTs began to work. Talking to the officers out of

Sam's earshot, Wolf said, "Appreciate it if you can get Sam under cover as soon as you can. Call Detective Mike McManus and tell him we need the SWAT team. Tell him Tom Wolf says another shooter showed."

"Shooter? This related to that guy who killed the Marine up here?"

"Affirmative. McManus will know what I'm talking about."

"Will do. What about you?"

"I'm not on the killer's list, Sergeant."

"I don't think it matters at this point. You'd be better off with us."

Wolf glanced at the showering sparks. "Thanks, but I promised Sam I'd keep his house safe. There's still a fire to fight."

"I'm calling it in."

"Thanks. And tell McManus he'd better hurry, this guy's not done."

Chapter 51

A stretcher came for McFadden. The EMTs stabilized him and lowered him on it. They were told they were to wheel him to an ambulance with policemen shielding him with every step. The sergeant tried a final word with Wolf. "You should think about this," he warned. "Look around you. Nighttime. All this smoke. Crews running around. Hard to tell who's out there, who's a friendly."

"I know," said Wolf. "I'll wait for the SWAT team."

"Okay, let's move, people."

Guns drawn, both officers formed a perimeter around the EMTs as they worked on McFadden. Wolf hovered beside the gurney. McFadden, in pain, pale despite the smeared ashes, groaned. "Sam, You're going with these gentlemen."

McFadden tried to lift himself. "But the fire. The house."

"Don't worry. I'll get a couple neighbors back on the hose. There's plenty of water yet. The fire crews are holding their own. They know the drill.

These officers will make sure you're safe."

Gripping Wolf's arm like a vise, McFadden panted, his accusing eyes boring into Wolf. "So much for your nozzle story. Tell me what really happened."

"He's here," said Wolf. "Our shooter set the fire as cover."

McFadden collapsed. "Got it. Watch out...Wolfman."

"Don't worry. We'll have the cops get you out of here."

"This might be the same killer...they warned about."

Ash drifted down. Wolf brushed it from McFadden's face. "Maybe his twin. Maybe a backup. He took a shot at me. Hit you. He'll want to finish it, Sam."

"Tell McManus."

"Already done. Still stash guns around the house, Sam?"

McFadden groaned. "Oh, man...I know you. Know what you're thinking."

"I am."

"Tell the..."

"Guns, Sam. Same old hiding places?"

McFadden's eyes filled with tears. "Oh, hell, Wolfman."

"Beretta. Entertainment center, top left hand drawer?"

Grimacing, McFadden nodded.

"Your office. The Sig. Still behind the flag display?"

Another nod, weaker.

"A done deal. Now git."

"Watch yourself, Tom Wolf." Sam glanced back and waved. Wolf vanished in the smoke, headed back inside Sam's home.

Chapter 52

Black ash, like weeping mascara, dripped from scorched tiled roofs, staining blistered stucco with sooty rivulets. Fire hoses crisscrossed front yards and streets in pools of water. The fire was being stymied but not without a stubborn rearguard action of its own. Pockets of flame hopscotched the gullies, consuming fresh fuel despite the fire crews' efforts. A towering cedar caught fire, then its twin, both lighting the night like huge tapers behind the lines. The ridge was holding but just barely, and not without cost.

Spotlights mounted on trucks focused on two homes, blackened, smoldering shells. Even in the faint light from burning brush, most houses bore blistered exteriors on at least three sides. Years of painstaking landscaping had been reduced to sodden ash. Wolf refueled the pump, hauled the hose to the surface, and handed the line to a firefighter. He had other work in mind.

Inside McFadden's house, Wolf tracked ash across the tiles to Sam's office, felt behind the flag case and found the loaded SIG Sauer. He pulled back on the slide, chambering a round. Despite thickening smoke hovering at eye level, he found the Beretta in the entertainment center's drawer and did the same. He slipped out the garage, pausing where Roderick had been killed. He knelt to touch the spot.

Semper Fi, Marine.

Heading next door to the abandoned house, Wolf darted from side to side, not about to offer a stationary target. He gained the garage. The firelight and spots from the trucks played havoc on the walls, creating dancing shadows. Behind him, fire crews alerted to the shooter by the cops, went about their task with an edgy awareness despite the threat. Wolf ran inside the ground floor, did a quick clearing of the space and edged into the back hall, a pistol in each hand. The kitchen space, a mess of tarps, paint buckets and ladders, was clear of the gunman as well. The entire downstairs was carpeted in stiff abandoned painters' cloths. He cleared each room in turn. That left the second floor.

I'd be up there, he thought. *High ground. He's got the advantage. Wait for backup, Wolf. More firepower. The SWAT team will show soon. But he could walk right by me. Right by the fire crews, the cops, everybody.*

Using the smoke as cover, Wolf crawled up the stairs, his back against the wall, the SIG Sauer out front, the Beretta pointed downstream just in case. He cleared all the rooms and headed downstairs, his senses on full alert. Scanning every corner, Wolf went back the way he had come, through the back hall, the kitchen, the garage.

Almost free of the garage, Wolf sensed a footfall behind him.

He dove to the floor, twisting, firing both pistols at a shadow in the doorway. Prone on the concrete, he fired again.

Too late.

Bullets ricocheted, chipping the garage's cement floor around him as he rolled, fired, rolled and fired. Wolf felt one round slam into his back like a sledgehammer, knocking the wind out of him. Stinging cordite filled his nostrils. The doorway was empty, the shadow gone.

Chapter 53

Wolf took a deep breath, felt the stabbing ache as if a rib had cracked.

Lucky shot, you bastard. He kept the SIG Sauer aimed at the doorway and crabbed on hands and knees to a wall, where he pushed himself to a standing position. With the pistol in his right hand, he leaned back, listening. Nothing. Wolf pushed away from the wall, leaving behind a smear of blood.

The Beretta. Where the hell is the Beretta? Musta' lost it when I rolled.

His breathing was shallow, his pain dull, manageable but building. *Lung hit*, he thought. *Got some time before shock sets in. You can move, Wolf. If you can move, you can shoot.* He headed to the beckoning doorway.

A random thought. *Sorry, Roderick, Sam, sorry I didn't get him.*

Clearing the door, Wolf swept his weapon back and forth. He followed footprints in the ash to the mansion's open back door. A shape crawled along a stone retaining wall overlooking the burning hill. Wolf steadied himself against the doorpost and fired. His prey rolled off the wall into smoke and flames.

Did I hit him?

Crouching, Wolf followed. Hoping to intercept his quarry, he kept to the wall until it met a metal railing marking McFadden's property. Despite his pain, Wolf lowered himself over the wall and dropped to the smoking ground on one knee. Hot to the touch, the soil smoldered, fire consuming what little vegetation was left.

Disoriented by drifting smoke, his vision limited, Wolf kept his back to the scorched wall. *He can't see me either.*

A cough. Louder. Someone gagging on the acrid fumes to Wolf's left. He tensed, his own lungs struggling. A shadow darted across his front, closer now. A man emerged ten feet away, a bandana held to his mouth, pistol in his right hand. Wolf fired twice. The shadow toppled, got up, fired back, missing, and melted away in the smoke.

Wolf risked following, stumbled in a narrow draw, and went down among charred skeletal brush. He climbed out, rocks scalding his knees and free hand. The effort sapped his strength. His breath, already shortened by the wound, came in short, raspy gulps of sooty air.

I know I hit him. Where is the sonofabitch?

Wolf clawed his way back to McFadden's lawn. *Don't stop. Don't sit down.* He reached the top of the ridge, staggering more than walking. He stayed on his feet, his head swiveling left and right to catch sight of the killer.

Not far away, mid-block on McFadden's street, an ambulance bathed in headlights, sat next to a fire rig. Firefighters clustered, some wearing oxygen masks, their faces covered in grime. Blinking to clear his blurred vision, Wolf headed in their direction, his movements ponderous, measured. He knew his body well, knew what was happening to him.

Adrenaline running low.

Shock setting in. Make it to the ambulance. They'll take it from there.

Neighbors, those who hadn't fled in cars, ran past him in both directions through the smoke. Their arms were filled with the oddest things: a favorite pillow, a child's stuffed animal, books, a framed oil. An antique armchair, an annoying small dog whining in full panic mode.

Just stuff, he thought. Breathing was painful, air coming in shallow gasps.

You're not dying...yet. Stay focused. Do not stop. Don't rest.

Mid-block, Wolf's eyes were drawn to a dark, gasping man propped with his back against a scorched car, arms at his side, eyes vacant. A face he didn't recognize, couldn't place. Wolf stopped, studying the man. The stranger wore a black T-shirt slick with blood. He swayed, staring at the man.

Wolf braved a closer look. Two ragged holes in the man's chest above the heart. Blood had congealed around the wounds. The man was dying. Wolf stepped away, tightening his grip on the SIG Sauer.

Was it possible?

Older than the man he had confronted descending McFadden's hillside and not the brazen visitor to the range. *No. That one was dead.*

But there was a familiarity.

"Sparrow?"

The question startled the mortally wounded man. Opening his eyes, he stared at Wolf, not fully comprehending who was speaking to him.

"Sparrow?"

The faintest of smiles spread across the man's lips.

"Tala?"

"What?"

"Tala...you came after all. I knew you would."

Wolf raised his weapon, centered it on the man's forehead.

"You are Sparrow...aren't you?"

In slow motion, the sitting man lifted his weapon, its suppressed muzzle pointed at the ground, useless. The effort taxed him. He grimaced. Tried again. Failed.

Steadying the SIG Sauer with both hands, Wolf centered the laser sight's red dot on Sparrow's forehead and squeezed the trigger as the man's eyes closed.

Chapter 54

Wolf heard the distinctive click.

"Commander Wolf, put down the gun! Commander. Do not fire."

A voice off to his left and behind. Running feet. The order repeated.

"Sir, do not fire your weapon. I say again, do not fire your weapon."

The same voice. "Commander Wolf, it's Detective Mike McManus. Hold the gun away from your body. I'll take it. You're hurt. You need immediate medical attention."

Wolf glanced down at the man sprawled against the car. "Sparrow," he rasped. He felt someone pry the pistol from his fingers. Two of the SWAT team crept forward, their M4's covering the assassin. Another team member retrieved the pistol from the dead man. Then, gentle hands on either side were steadying Wolf. Two fire department EMTs in neon yellow jacket and pants approached him.

One said, "We've got a stretcher."

Wolf waved away the help. "Prefer to...walk out."

One glance at his determined patient told the paramedic not to argue. "Okay. We'll get you to the ambulance, sir. Come with us."

Wolf put one foot in front of the other, following obediently behind one medic, the other supporting him. McManus trailed with a heavily armed SWAT team member. When they reached the ambulance Wolf said, "Don't want to sit." He grimaced. "I go down, I won't get up again. Lung shot. Leaking blood in... chest cavity. Hard to breathe."

Despite his protest Wolf was eased onto the running board for the lead medic to do a trauma assessment. He felt scissors run up the back of his sweat-soaked T-shirt, splitting it.

"Name's Wolf," he wheezed.

"I'm Brian," said the gloved medic, running his hands over Wolf's torso, scalp, and arms. He nodded at his partner. "That's Eddie."

Wolf nodded at the introductions. "Okay, Brian, Eddie... I'm probably in...compensated shock. Shallow breaths. Swallowed a lot of bad smoke. Mouth tastes like...a campfire. Nose full of ash. How about some water?"

"I'm impressed. You a doctor, sir?"

Wolf shook his head. "Negative."

McManus, on the fringe, interrupted. "That's Commander Wolf you're working on, Brian. As in Navy SEAL, retired."

"Outstanding," said the medic, staring at Wolf. "Amazing, sir. You sustained a bad hit. Right, upper back. You have deep scalp lacerations as well. Burns and possibly smoke inhalation. We'll take it from here."

Handed a bottle of water, Wolf rinsed his mouth and spit streams of soot at his feet, then did it again. Dousing his blackened face with fresh water, he blinked, flushing ash from his eyes and nose.

Brian, the lead medic, swabbed Wolf's back, cleansing the area around the bullet wound. His partner, Eddie, taped a gauze patch over the entry wound to prevent air from entering the chest cavity, while allowing air to exit. He checked Wolf's blood pressure, pulse, and oxygen saturation levels.

"This should help," Brian said, slipping a clear plastic mask over Wolf's nose and mouth. Wolf listened to the paramedics run through their checklist.

"Lung sounds absent on the right. Diminished on the left."

The pressure on Wolf's heart had increased, along with the pain.

"We need to dart his chest," said Brian, opening his equipment bag. "Eddie, give him two milligrams of Versed."

Dazed but alert, Wolf barely felt the IV poke his arm.

Eddie said, "Two milligrams on board."

"Roger that." Brian knelt in front of Wolf. "I'm going to perform a procedure to help you breathe. I'll be honest, Commander, it's going to hurt."

Nodding wearily, Wolf mumbled through the mask. "Been there, done that. Do your worst, mister."

Brian readied a large bore needle sheathed with a soft rubber catheter and described what he was about to do.

"The gunshot wound collapsed your lung and trapped air inside your chest, sir. The pressure is squeezing your heart. We're putting a needle into your chest to allow you to breathe. We're giving you meds to ease your pain."

Wolf eyed the needle without flinching. "Do it."

Eddie nicked a small incision between the second and third ribs below Wolf's clavicle and backed away to allow his partner to insert the needle. A quick spurt of pink foam shot from the incision, followed by another. Working the catheter into the slit, Brian withdrew the needle as his fellow EMT began staunching dribbling blood with large gauze pads. Wolf gulped air, pushing out more blood with each breath. The paramedics attached a one-way valve to the rubber tube and taped it down on Wolf's bare chest.

Despite splattering himself with bloody bubbles, a relieved Wolf flashed a thumbs up to the medics. While they worked, McManus stepped in front of Wolf with his questions. "Was that your shooter?"

Wolf pulled away the mask, tried to turn his head. "Sparrow."

"You're positive?"

"It's him. Or someone just like him."

"Was he alone?"

Wolf nodded. "Think so."

The medics painted his burns with ointment and taped temporary dressings in place, then picked at his bleeding scalp.

McManus said, "You got him, Commander."

Wolf's eyes filled. "He shot...Sam."

"Yes, we know."

"Tried...to kill me."

"Tried is the key word, Commander."

"I'm tired."

"You should be. Helluva night."

At Brian's insistence, Wolf replaced the mask and raised a hand. "Sam?"

"He's doing okay," said McManus. "Reggie was called. She's on her way."

Mumbling through the mask, Wolf said, "Ah, good...Let him know...about...Sparrow Number Two."

"Tell you what," said McManus, "let him hear it from you."

Shooing McManus from their patient, the EMTs wrapped Wolf in a blanket and put him in the ambulance along with a prone firefighter. At his insistence, Wolf was not forced to lie down on the gurney during the ride to the hospital.

Chapter 55

Scripps Mercy Hospital, three days later

Wolf overtook McFadden in the hall. Both of them wore hospital pajamas, blue robes, and non-skid slippers. Tethered to IV poles, the pair shuffled in tandem. Wolf's scalp was shaved in spots. Three days of blond beard sprinkled with gray added to his grizzled look.

"Hey, Sam," croaked Wolf, "you've looked better. Seen a mirror lately?"

"Morning, Wolfman, you peaked long ago yourself."

"Where's Reggie?"

"Should be here shortly. Really, how you doing?"

Wolf grinned. "Feeling like I could go ten rounds. You?"

Patting his butt, McFadden said, "Taking it day by day. I feel like a pin cushion with all the antibiotics they're giving me."

"I feel your pain, Sam."

"I'm getting out tomorrow."

"Really? Then I want out too," said Wolf. "I'm not a happy camper. I should go AWOL."

"You want out? Talk to your doctor."

Wolf mumbled something unintelligible.

"Reggie stopped by yesterday," said McFadden. She's been a trouper. Taken over the job of cleaning up the house. Amazing, after all she went through."

"She's an Iron Lady," said Wolf. "Probably good for her to focus on you and getting your place back in shape."

McFadden bent over a drinking fountain, lapping at the cold water. "She even has the painting crew back at work. Said she's doing something with beige and eggshell off-white after all. The pool guesthouse came through fine. Doesn't smell like smoke at all, she says. Your gear is safe. We hope you'll stay and do your rehab there."

"Thanks," said Wolf. "That will make things easier once the docs sign off.

I've got places to go and people I need to see."

McFadden spotted a trio of men in suits headed their way. "Here come McManus and Mathis again. The M and M team."

Wolf said, "They've got a Hoover suit along for good measure. Hope this goes better than last time."

The two halted in the hallway and watched the shift supervisor intercept McManus and his two companions.

"Looks like we're finally getting our de-briefing," said McFadden.

"Our second debriefing," groused Wolf. "Not that I'm keeping score, but I'm ready for some good news."

The senior nurse, a tall no-nonsense brunette in baggy scrubs, came after the two. "Commander, you and Major McFadden have visitors. You can use our staff conference room. I'll show you the way."

"I told you, it's Tom and Sam," complained Wolf.

She smiled. "Forgot. Dad was career Navy. The rank thing is ingrained in me, I guess."

McFadden laughed. "See, you remind her of her father, Wolfman."

"Is that some sort of private joke between you two?" she said.

Wolf glared at McFadden. "Don't pay any attention to him. Okay, lead on, Nurse Ratched."

"That is so overused," she deadpanned. "Follow me."

"And that is so Army," he said.

Herding their IV poles alongside, the two shuffled into a sun-filled conference room where McManus and Mathis waited with their FBI liaison.

Wolf came in the door, parked his IV, and claimed a chair opposite.

"Gentlemen, good morning. So nice of you to come."

McFadden followed, nodding to the lawmen. "Hope you're here to brighten our day." He and Wolf waited. The visitors took seats, each with a folder in hand.

"Don't add to our pain," warned Wolf. "We're already at level seven."

"Not our purpose," said McManus. "We're here to tidy up more details. We learned some interesting things since we last spoke."

"Last time we talked it was a lot hotter," said Wolf. The men laughed.

"Last time we talked, my friend and I were under serious medication," said McFadden. "We may not have remembered everything you told us. You might have to repeat yourselves for our benefit."

"Not a problem," Mathis said. "This is Special Agent Trey Dickerson. He stopped in to check on you earlier but you both were a little under the weather."

Groans, not laughter, from Wolf and McFadden.

"He's familiar with the case, start to finish," added Mathis. Dickerson shot a quick smile at them. "Appreciate what both of you have been through. Sorry it ended the way it did... aside from your surviving life-threatening injuries, of course. My colleagues are grateful, as we all are, that you came through with flying colors. Thank goodness for first-rate medical care."

Wolf settled his arms on the table, eyeing the agent. "Was it Sparrow?"

"Yes. You got the right man this time around. We all agree on that."

"Finally," interrupted McManus. "We weren't the only ones who thought Reggie finished him that first time around."

"We'll get to that," said Dickerson. "

McManus broke in. "She did a remarkable thing, Sam. Very brave."

"And the women you told us were found in the wreckage of the van that hit the fire engine at the park entrance," said Wolf. "Either of them someone you were looking for?"

"Affirmative. Positive ID on one, Tala."

Wolf scowled. "The other woman. Who was she?"

Dickerson deferred to McManus, who said, "We're pretty sure she was one of Biggie Pacheco's gang. Looks like the two of them accompanied Sparrow to the lake that night."

"But you made a positive ID on Tala?" said McFadden.

"Affirmative. Her aunt identified tattoos on the body. The deceased also matched surveillance video from your range cameras. And Bob tagged her through her association with a local martial arts training center. Full name was Tala Maria Roxas. Definitely mixed up with Biggie Pacheco's safe house network. The ME says she suffered multiple stab wounds, though the crash finished the job."

"Mike," said Mathis, "tell them about the second woman."

"Right. Killed instantly in that collision. Not much left to work with according to the medical examiner but they did get a preliminary match using tattoos. Gotta love these gangbangers and their body art. Doc says she was shot. We found the weapon in the wreckage. Tala apparently fired it. Bullets match," said McManus. "That night's chronology is a mess right now. We'll sort it out eventually. We hauled Biggie's ass down to the morgue to ID the second woman but he claimed he didn't know her. More of his bullshit."

Mathis snorted, "He turned himself in around twenty-two hundred hours that evening. Convenient, huh? Obvious he was distancing himself from what went down. He's lawyered up, but we'll confirm the second woman's identity and tie her to the sonofabitch without his help."

"Why do you think he turned himself in?" said Wolf.

"His lawyer's story is he was afraid to show on the streets when we were looking for him. Then there was more bullshit about not wanting to be hit by other gangbangers. It's bogus. We think he left it to this Sparrow guy to kill Sam, then get taken out by our guys. That confuses our theory about what the two women were there for. But we're going with that for now."

McFadden said, "So, who was the real Sparrow? Which one of these guys, the first one or this last guy? After all this is settled, what do you know about them?"

Yielding to the fed again, McManus said, "You have the floor."

Dickerson opened his folder and handed out sets of stapled sheets. As the men read, he painted a portrait of the second assassin. "The guy who came with fire is the real deal. Sparrow is...or was, his *nom de guerre*. The authorities in Manila are familiar with his work but not his real name or background, if you can believe that. We have no paper trail. No hits with fingerprints. No DNA. Interpol had nothing.

Our killer was obviously a homegrown Philippines product. Never left the islands as far as anyone can figure except for this one time, and that only last week.

He shuffled some papers and continued reading. "This guy flew under Manila's radar for a long time. There are rumors he was one of the more successful of the contract killers for hire. And believe me, there are a lot of his kind out there. Sparrow was always contacted by word of mouth. Elusive. No ID on the first guy yet. We think he was sent ahead or was acting on his own as a contract killer. Manila was sent photos and fingerprints. They're still trying to piece together his part in this."

"How many people do they think this second guy killed?" said Wolf.

Dickerson consulted his notes. "Their National Bureau of Investigation pegs the number at around forty-five. Three-quarters of those political. Likely more."

"All from one guy?" McFadden let out a low whistle as he studied the sheet.

"One bad dude," said Mathis.

"Busy," said Wolf.

Glancing up from the sheets, McFadden said, "And the why? I think I know the answer, but what do the FBI and our local police think?"

"Are you all on the same page?" said Wolf.

The three lawmen nodded in unison. Dickerson said, "I defer to Detectives McManus and Mathis for their theory."

McFadden said, "Okay, then let's start with you, Mike."

Chapter 56

"We think," said McManus, looking at McFadden, "that after all is said and done, you were the intended target."

"Not Reggie?"

McManus rubbed his jaw. "Sam, we can't sit here and single you out with one hundred percent certainty, of course. And given your wife's family history in the Philippines it's a possibility she may have been targeted as well. But all three of us now agree killing you was Sparrow's primary mission."

Puzzled, Wolf said, "Why then would this first guy go after Reggie?"

"Boils down to a calculated guess on our part," said McManus. "We think she may have been a target of opportunity that day. The killer was after you. Guess he thought he could set up and wait."

Wolf said, "Sure, but Roderick upset that plan."

McManus glanced at Mathis and Dickerson but found no help there. He shrugged. "Best we can do, Sam."

Wolf said, "With the women and Sparrow dead and Biggie playing dumb you have no way to confirm your theory."

"Afraid so," said Dickerson. "But we think it's a reasonable assumption."

"Any idea who ordered these two Sparrow guys to make the hit on Sam?"

Dickerson brightened. "That we can pinpoint with some accuracy. Our man in Manila was told that of the four men who attended the original meeting where the contract was discussed, only three are still alive. Of that number, only one, Felix Mendoza, has a connection to Zamboanga in Mindanao."

Leaning forward to focus on the fed, McFadden said, "Do you know if Mendoza is connected to the *Kuretong Balelong*?"

"He is," said Dickerson. "Their top man in Zamboanga."

Spreading his arms, McFadden said, "That's it! He's what they'd call, *Papa Manong*. In my book that makes him the logical choice as the one who arranged for Sparrow to take on this mission."

Wolf spoke up. "All Sam's problems originated in Zamboanga. So it's logical that Mendoza would be the source for this killer-for-hire plot. But did he send both these guys?"

All three went to poker-face mode.

Their silence provoked a frown from McFadden. "Can you say," he said, "with any assurance, that this ends it?"

A long unsettling pause descended. The trio facing Wolf and McFadden shifted in their seats.

"Speaking for the Bureau," said Dickerson, "I cannot guarantee that."

McManus threw up his hands. "We don't have the intel to disagree."

His eyes narrowing, McFadden said, "So, Reggie and I will have to do the best we can to get on with our lives."

"It's the only advice we can offer you, Sam," said McManus.

"Small comfort, Mike."

Mathis said, "I can promise that we'll do our best to make sure you're not on someone's list. The chief said to tell you the department will monitor the situation and stay in touch with our friends in the Bureau."

Dickerson folded his hands in front of him. "I will pursue this with our man in Manila. We've sent photos and fingerprints of both killers to Manila. The Bureau will make every effort to find out who these two were. We'll try to put a name to them. There may yet be a way to put this to rest."

"Small comfort," huffed Wolf.

"Best we can do, gentlemen."

Spotting Reggie waiting in the hallway, McFadden pushed from the table and got to his feet. "Appreciate the wrap up, gentlemen. Now if you'll excuse me." He hobbled from the room, one hand gripping the IV stand.

Wolf sat for a moment longer, then rose as well. "If you are ever able to sort out this cluster fuck then let us know. Personally, I think you'll be trying to make connections and assigning blame for a long time. I don't envy your task."

The lawmen stood. McManus said, "Commander Wolf, I want to say that we appreciate your help in running Sparrow...the real one...to ground. It was a courageous thing you did."

Wolf paused in the doorway. "If you're convinced I got the right guy, so be it.

But whatever I did, I did for Sam and Reggie."

"I understand. But thanks for putting yourself on the line."

"We're in the same boat. You do it...every day."

Chapter 57

Lotus Garden Hotel, Padre Faura Street, Manila

Agent John Stiles, the American Embassy's Legat—the FBI's eyes and ears in the Philippines capital—had baited his ambush with a promise of rum. Between drumming fingers on the table and reading his wristwatch every thirty seconds, Stiles was beginning to wonder if his meeting with Colonel Rojas was a bad idea after all. The day before, a clandestine call from a trusted mid-level acquaintance in the police had undermined his confidence in Rojas as an unimpeachable source. Armed with a confidential report, Stiles toyed with the idea of exposing the officer or continuing the relationship. He was on his own. Washington knew nothing of his plans to confront Rojas. The colonel had survived the careers of the previous six legats by playing the agents like his personal instruments. Certain his bosses in Washington would object, Stiles kept his strategy to himself. It was a risky move.

You burned me, Colonel, thought Stiles. *Turnabout is fair play, though you, sir, wouldn't know the meaning of the word 'fairness' or 'loyalty.'*

Stiles spotted Rojas crossing the marble entry in full military finery, strutting like a prized cock in a *sabong* ring. As though the man could sniff the good stuff, Rojas headed straight for the tumbler of Tanduay across from Stiles. Practiced plastic smile in place, the American rose, extending his hand. "Colonel, so good of you to come." The two shook hands.

Rojas eyed the rum. "Ah, you know the way to my heart, Agent Stiles."

"Just a token of appreciation, Colonel. Why the dress uniform?"

"Ah, an awards ceremony for a colleague. Not that he deserved it, mind you."

Stiles oozed sincerity. "Striking outfit, sir. It becomes you."

Rojas tested the rum. "Excellent. Of course, women like a man in uniform do they not? That has been my experience."

"My linen suit pales in comparison, sir."

"So, Mister Stiles, to business. Your message had an urgency about it."

"Of course. Remember our conversation about the assassin called Sparrow?"

Another draw on the rum. "Yes, of course. It is a rumor at headquarters that this man was found out. Killed in the midst of an assassination attempt in San Diego, California, yes?"

Stiles smiled despite the man's duplicity. "Your sources are impeccable, Colonel. Yes, this Sparrow fellow was killed while attempting to murder one of our citizens. Apparently, he chose the wrong man to kill."

"Good. You confirm his death then?"

"I can, sir."

"I hope my information helped in some way, hasten his death."

"Indeed it did."

"I do my best to help a valued ally."

Stiles pulled a folded piece of paper from his breast pocket. "Odd circumstances, however. Do you recall my initial astonishment that this man was allowed to leave the Philippines within twenty-four hours of assassinating JuJu Cruz?"

Another sip of Tanduay and a wary look from Rojas. "Perhaps. He was a practiced master of disguise. He slipped away before we were aware of his involvement in Cruz's murder."

Stiles leaned in, speaking conspiratorially. "I have been told by a trusted source in the police that this 'Second Sparrow' if you will, had help in both the killing of JuJu Cruz and his immediate flight to America."

Rojas bristled. "An outrageous lie. Who says such a thing?"

"There's more, sir. This source also claims that Sparrow Two was sent on his way with the expectation that he would be killed by the police in San Diego."

The colonel's indignation, real enough to any eavesdropper, did not impress Stiles. "It seems that your country solved several problems at once, sir. You allowed a known killer to eliminate a major criminal, JuJu Cruz, then sent this same assassin on his way, thus ridding your nation of this killer. You then profited from his death in America so that he didn't live to confirm the story. Very convenient. And the dead man has no identity, no record, no history other than what your agency credits him with. Mysterious but quite tidy don't you agree?"

"An insulting fantasy. Surely, you cannot believe such lies."

"Oh, and there's a footnote to this episode. I've been told the first man who entered California to kill one of my countrymen was someone named Leon Padilla, a known associate who acted as a go-between for this Sparrow. Fingerprints sent from our field office in San Diego matched those on file here. These are your agency's own records. You, sir, did not see fit to furnish me with these facts though I asked you to."

"Really, who is feeding you these wild tales?"

"Officials who seem to think cooperation is a two-way street, Colonel."

"You are being duped, Agent Stiles. You are naive to believe this."

Stiles threw up his hands. "Who knows? My source intimates that JuJu Cruz was killed in order to seize control from him of the lucrative *jueteng* racket. This illegal gambling enterprise now passes to someone with government connections, I'm told."

Rojas stood up, his faced contorted in controlled fury. "This insinuation is a blot on my character, sir. It cannot be tolerated. You have insulted our nation with these wild tales. I will not be part of this. If you come to your senses and apologize I will consider the matter behind us. If you persist in this matter I will no longer work with you. Good day, sir."

With the threat hanging in the air, Rojas tucked his officer's hat under his arm and marched from the hotel's bar, his mahogany face set in an angry frown.

Stiles sat back, unmoved by the colonel's blatant evasion. He imagined the digging Rojas would do to unearth the "police source" that had furnished the damaging revelations. In fact, there was no single secret source. Stiles had spent painstaking hours assembling evidence of government complicity from dozens of tips—a word here, a phone call, a letter, a conflicted policeman, and a junior military man ashamed of his superiors' malfeasance. Today, he had gambled big on instinct by facing down the duplicitous Rojas over the Sparrow Affair and had won.

Even as he sat there looking at Rojas's abandoned rum, Stiles knew the anonymous letter he had sent to Manila's three biggest tabloids detailing Sparrow's bloody mission would soon bear fruit. Washington would be horrified to know of his subterfuge but he would say nothing about its origins. Besides, the intrigue surrounding the Sparrow Affair was the kind of corrupt circus Manila media fed on daily.

Rojas, ever a thorn in Stiles's side, would be preoccupied for a long time, looking over his shoulder and wondering who was watching. The thought pleased him. There were other nationals Stiles could cultivate— Honest sources as well as those with an ax to grind. He would not miss the spurned colonel.

Chapter 58

Epilogue

In Zamboanga, long knives came for Alberto *"Razor"* Mendoza in the night.

He heard them first kill his chauffeur in the courtyard, then his bodyguard on his threshold. Mendoza's housekeeper later told the police there were three assassins, heavily armed and determined. What she did not tell them was that once the sentinels were dead she let the killers inside the house and showed them Mendoza's bedroom. He did not go quietly. Managing to kill one attacker with a gun before it jammed, Mendoza mortally wounded a second with a butterfly knife. The police, warned of the plot in advance, had not interfered that night; preferring instead to wait until summoned by the disloyal housekeeper. The surviving killer, shot by police after surrendering, had ties to JuJu Cruz's *barkada*. After being hospitalized and recovering, he was released for unexplained reasons and disappeared. With Mendoza's death the basket of serpents that was the *Kuratong Baleleng* emptied its poisonous contents across Zamboanga in internecine warfare, adding to the city's agony.

Recalled from his Manila posting six months hence, the FBI's John Stiles thought his career ruined. He needn't have worried. His motives in uncovering the government's role in the Sparrow Affair were never discovered. His replacement, a careerist, ignored Stiles's advice and initiated contact with Rojas in the first week of taking office. The colonel, full of charm and intimacy, renewed his ties with the American embassy by taking the new legat under his wing.

Biggie Pacheco, held for questioning in what San Diego's media dubbed *The Sparrow Murders*, declared he was innocent of the murder of Manny Ramos and any connections to attempts on the McFaddens. His lawyer skillfully shifted focus for Ramos's death onto both Sparrows. Also charged in Cesar's killing and immolation, Biggie evaded responsibility by again shifting the focus on Tala and the first Sparrow—the irony being his actual innocence in that case. Despite his lawyer's maneuvering, he was convicted under California's Penal Code 32 for harboring fugitives and sentenced to one year in the county jail. Convinced Pacheco was literally getting away with murder, both the feds and the state pooled information in order to go after him on RICO charges. He was a marked man and knew it.

Tala's aunt played the "memory-loss card" and evaded culpability for her hidden role in the safe-house setup. A slap on the wrist for housing code violations was the closest she came to jeopardy.

Detectives Mike McManus and Bob Mathis had coveted letters of commendation added to their personnel files. They continued their high-profile careers. Mathis eventually transferred to the San Diego Police Department's Homicide Cold Case task force.

Sam McFadden and Reggie healed, the result of his iron constitution and her inner resilience. McFadden's rehabilitation regime, which Reggie oversaw with all the compassion of a drill sergeant, succeeded. Mobility in his left arm and shoulder was completely restored. His business continues to prosper. Insurance money covered the ravages of the earlier assault and the subsequent fire to their home.

The ridge above Lake Miramar, scene of horrific damage that fateful night, also recovered. Creative landscaping, new stucco, and fresh paint went a long way to restore what once was. The home adjacent to McFadden's survived the fire and a contractor's lawsuit, becoming a showplace. The blackened hills put forth new plants, the scorched earth blooms with life. Like much of the state, there remains a desperate need for rain and Lake Miramar's level remains low. Boaters, cyclists, runners, and walkers continue to flock to the park. From the heights, the views, never threatened, remain stunning.

Wolf amazed his doctors with his ability to heal. Spending time with the McFaddens strengthened his bond with them. On indefinite leave from his post at DARPA—the Defense Advanced Research Projects Agency—he has become a semi-permanent resident in the guesthouse. He swims daily, practices Tai Chi routines with willing pupil, Reggie, and has taken up running again with his doctor's permission. Wolf's personal rehabilitation regimen includes self-prescribed long, isolated weekends at the beach with Crystal Hamm, the television reporter. For this part of his recovery, he did not seek his doctor's permission.

Riding a borrowed Sportster, he occasionally joins Walt Jonski and the Marine veterans of HMM-361's *Flying Tigers* on their rides. It is a practice Wolf's doctor frowns on, despite his patient's pledge to wear a helmet.

www.ingramcontent.com/pod-product-compliance
Lightning Source LLC
LaVergne TN
LVHW051513080426
835509LV00017B/2051